TESTIMONIALS

"Dr. Cora's latest work, *Leading Under Pressure* is a crisp, clear, insightful essential for every senior executive's tool box. In it, she presents invaluable information drawn from her years in the trenches as a doctor, coach and consultant in a highly user-friendly, and inspirational manner... a must-read for any manager in today's corporate environment!"

- **Cathleen R. Pratt, President & CEO,**
  The Revenue Generators

"Entrepreneurs rarely have the opportunity to openly discuss the unique stress they experience in their lives. I was very impressed by your ability to immediately resonate with a group of business owners from around the world. I truly believe you made a difference in each of our lives that day."

- **Calvin Carter, Business Owner**
  Entrepreneurs' Organization Regional Director,
  North America

"Gaby has been a wonderful coach/mentor in working through very difficult family problems in our business. Her insight into interaction between brothers who are also business partners has been a tremendous help to me as I have taken brothers and cousins and assigned them to areas where their best talents can be used to move the business ahead without alienating them or causing an impasse."

- **Gary Wells, CEO,**
  Blue Bunny World Presidents' Organization Member

"Women Business Enterprises and business women in general live under all sorts of pressure and perform daily balancing acts. Some of us have developed skills to help us cope with our roles as business and community leaders, mothers, sisters and daughters. Many of us need help - that's where *Leading Under Pressure* comes in - a great resource for us all. Thanks, Gaby for your insight, your thoroughness and your ability to help us not only define, but refine what we are looking for and what we can expect."

- **Nancy Allen, President & CEO,
  WBDC Florida Affiliate of the Women's Business
  Enterprise National Council**

"In her book *Leading Under Pressure*, Dr. Gabriela Corá depicts and addresses the most important challenges that Executives and Corporate Professionals face in their daily practices. The content of this book is as useful to the busy business executives as it is to physicians at large, and especially to psychiatrists and other mental health professionals.

In this text, Dr. Corá demonstrates extremely well the role of stress and burnt-out vis-à-vis medical and psychiatric conditions. Obviously, this book is essential for everyone interested in the topic of health and well-being."

- **Pedro Ruiz, M.D., Past President,
  American Psychiatric Association**

"Dr. Corá - Thank you, your presentation was lively and the concept easy to grasp; our group appreciated your talk on Life-Work Management tremendously!

On a personal note the information was very timely as I've realized that the only way to approach life and work is to apply your concept of "AIM / IAM." So I'm consciously making changes in my life that will allow me to maintain focused on what my goals are so that I can accomplish them and enjoy life!!!"

-   **Ana Alleguez, President,**
    Alleguez Architecture, Inc. Women Presidents'
    Organization Member

"First and foremost it was comforting after our initial discussion knowing that we had someone competent to turn to in helping deal with sensitive issues that can arise from time to time. Since these issues can develop rather quickly, the sooner they can be dealt with the better. I was very impressed with Gaby's response time and the cooperation to work around the schedule of all parties involved.

In addition, Gaby always made everyone feel very comfortable with expressing their feelings or concerns. All of her advice was always well thought out, and presented in a professional, non-demeaning manner. This could be very difficult to do if you are not an expert in knowing how to effectively communicate with people and have the experience in solving tough issues that can come about in businesses. We felt very fortunate to have met Gaby and made her be part of our team."

-   **Terry W. Claus, President,**
    Home Financing Center
    Miami, Florida

"Your New Life Business Plan has been a tremendous value in 'redirecting' my life in the manner in which I want it to go versus losing control to life circumstances. After three plus years I am still using it as my foundation to move forward with my daily life. You should spread the word about this great tool that you developed as it will assist many!"

- **Regional Account Manager,**
  Fortune 50

LEADING UNDER PRESSURE

MAXIMIZE YOUR HEALTH WHILE BUILDING YOUR WEALTH

GABRIELA CORÁ, MD, MBA

Published by:
The Executive Health & Wealth Institute, Inc.
Address: 8101 Biscayne Boulevard, Suite 516, Miami, FL 33138, USA
Telephone: 1-866-762-7632
Website: www.ExecutiveHealthWealth.com
Also available in digital e- book format ISBN 978-0-9766645-2-9
For internet book purchases, please visit: www.LeadingUnderPressure.com
For bulk orders of this book contact us at: Resources@ExecutiveHealthWealth.com

Cover and Interior Design by:
Prime Concepts Group Publishing (PCG)
Website: www.PrimeConcepts.com
Cover design: Jeff Sparks, PCG
Interior design: Chad Fatino, PCG

We thank Roy Llera Photography for Dr. Gabriela Corá's pictures

Publisher's Cataloging-in-Publication

    Corá, Gabriela.
       Leading under pressure : maximize your health while
    building your wealth / Gabriela Corá.
       p. cm.
       LCCN 2008905995
       ISBN-13: 978-0-9766645-0-5
       ISBN-10: 0-9766645-0-X
       ISBN-13: 978-0-9766645-1-2
       ISBN-10: 0-9766645-1-8
       [etc.]

       1. Executives--Health and hygiene. 2. Health.
    3. Job stress. I. Title.

RA777.65.C67 2008   613'.088658
             QBI08-600218

TABLE OF CONTENTS

ACKNOWLEDGMENTS 1

INTRODUCTION 3

CHAPTER 1 9
Leading Under Pressure

CHAPTER 2 15
The Wellbeing & Stress Continua

CHAPTER 3 19
Pressure Points

CHAPTER 4 25
Facts About Acute And Chronic Stress

CHAPTER 5 31
The Stress Response & Resilience

CHAPTER 6 35
Medical Illnesses With A Stress Component

CHAPTER 7 39
Facts About Depression

CHAPTER 8 45
Facts About Anxiety

CHAPTER 9 49
Medical Interventions For Depression And
Anxiety Disorders

CHAPTER 10 . . . . **53**
Facts About Performance And Productivity

CHAPTER 11 . . . . **57**
Individual Health & Wealth Assessment
& Strategies

CHAPTER 12 . . . . **73**
Organizational Health & Wealth Assessment
& Strategies

CHAPTER 13 . . . . **87**
Maximize Your Performance and Productivity:
Effective Strategies To Manage Your Daily Routine

CHAPTER 14 . . . . **97**
Maximize Your Performance and Productivity:
Effective Strategies to Manage Crises

CHAPTER 15 . . . . **101**
Effective Strategies to Maximize Your Health &
Wellbeing: The Four Pillars Of Biological Health

BONUS CHAPTER **107**
Individual Health & Organizational Health

BIOGRAPHY **113**

ADDITIONAL WORKS **117**

CORPORATE CONSULTING SERVICES **123**

ACKNOWLEDGEMENTS

I would like to express my deepest gratitude to the many people with whom I have worked and learned from to produce the ideas and strategies that are presented in this book.

To Eduardo Locatelli, MD, MPH, my husband, friend and colleague. My special thanks to Eduardo for patiently designing the graphs.

To Natalia and Marcos, our children. My special thanks to Natalia, for patiently assisting me with editing this work.

To my colleagues, mentors, and guides.

To my clients and patients, who have trusted me to assist them over the years. You have been my source of inspiration, as I have learned from you.

To my parents, Rosita and Ettore, and family, Vanesa, Pablo, Ellen, and Vero. To all my friends.

INTRODUCTION

If you feel like the professional juggler, multi-tasking and wishing for three extra pairs of hands, a new brain or if you are plotting to order a couple of clones of yourself, this book is meant for you. *Leading Under Pressure* summarizes the many challenges executives, professionals, entrepreneurs, and road-warriors face in the current fast-paced corporate craze, where exceptional expectations in productivity and performance are the norm, but where there is little guidance in how to do it all, perfectly well, and at once. And, of course, where you are also expected to succeed at everything in each and every aspect of your life, leading your team to achieve the best, contending against competing groups, and enhancing your family's wellbeing, again, perfectly well and at once! *Leading Under Pressure* represents many hours of work as a corporate consultant, clinical researcher, and medical doctor. It condenses and translates hours of interaction: identifying, conceptualizing, planning, and strategically resolving challenges, incorporating lessons learned from the bench to the bedside to the workplace!

Millions around the world are thinking, planning, and scheming how to stretch a 24 hour-day into an endless and productive working day, an endless loop of "useful" time. The problem is not that busy executives are lazy, that they want to cut corners or do not want to do their job. On the contrary, the problem is that executives face the daily quandary of finding new ways to thrive in order to achieve higher goals, with increased competition, progressively limited resources, and the same manpower. Busy executives now experience the need to work more hours to maintain their lifestyles. As they move up or across the corporate ladder, they find escalating challenges to remain level-headed, even-tempered, and able to balance all their difficulties, all at once. Corporate executives find themselves needing to do more with less.

As a consultant, entrepreneur, physician, executive, researcher, author, speaker, spouse, and mother, I can appreciate the incredible challenges and feats that others face in their daily responsibilities as I continue to face and master these challenges myself. *Leading Under Pressure* is a humble attempt to share my lessons-learned, to provide for processed information applied in a rational and practical way, proactively designing a master plan that will last a lifetime. *Leading Under Pressure* is intended to assist leading executives as they continue to move within the corporate structure effectively and steadily. As they implement their plan, executives are readily able to anticipate challenges and avoid damaging situations. As executives become their own guides, they are able to maximize their productivity and performance, balancing and integrating healthy lifestyles, building powerful relationships and achieving ultimate wellbeing. Please, join me in *Leading Under Pressure*.

Gabriela Corá, MD, MBA
Miami, Florida, 2008.

I had just returned from a US-based business trip and hopped into my next international flight to join my family. I was flying alone, on my way to a family gathering in South America, sitting in a buck seat in economy class. A man came to sit next to me.

He was forcing a smile: he had experienced several problems with his connecting flights and he had "ended-up" in coach, annoyed he missed his first class seat on another flight. He was not looking forward to an overnight flight on a less desirable seat. While at 5'6", I do not experience leg space problems on most airlines, at over 6 feet tall, my fellow passenger wasn't happy.

We started chit-chatting and he became slightly more enthusiastic as he described his business: he was a broker and investor, partnering with US and European investors in purchasing land in beautiful Patagonia. I listened carefully as he described his business activities. He seemed to become even more interested when he realized I was quite familiar with the hype as well as knowledgeable of the Southern cone's socio-economic culture.

Then came my turn to share what I did for a living. I immediately perceived a significant shift back to his initial tension when I spoke: "I have two practices: on the one hand, I practice medicine on a part-time basis. I am a psychiatrist and my area of expertise is mood and anxiety disorders. In my work as a doctor, I was seeing many wealthy business owners and executives. In spite of their piles of gold, there was a deep sense of failure; for them, it was never enough, and many felt unhappy with their lives. Many felt they were working 24/7 and felt like they needed to work even more. Most were pumping coffee throughout the course of the day to stay awake, and many were having alcoholic drinks or taking hypnotics at night to go to bed. Some were already taking prescribed stimulants to work even more hours throughout the course of the day, whereas others were taking stimulants to stay awake a second night within a week for extra work. Many regretted missed opportunities to spend quality time with their loved ones. More so, when they had the time with their family and friends, they did not enjoy it. They were experiencing a deep disconnection. They thought how much they missed them when they were not together, yet, when they were in their presence, they could not feel happy but kept thinking about the "things" they needed to do for work. Many were coming to see me burnt-out, depleted of energy, with medical conditions such as gastro-intestinal problems, neck pain and tension, or migraine headaches. Many had already visited emergency rooms thinking they were having a heart attack when they were having a panic attack instead."

I could see my flight companion turn pale, hypnotized by my story. I continued: "So, I realized the medical premise in our healthcare system did not necessarily address all of these issues at the core but, instead, the system was attempting to treat the obvious symptoms but did not address the underlying problems that produced the symptoms. I have been very interested in the medical and business interface for years, I had even decided to further my education by adding an MBA to my medical doctorate degree, and so, this is how The Executive Health & Wealth Institute came to existence. My area of expertise as a consultant is in individual and organizational health and wealth: I assist corporate executives and entrepreneurs as they lead under pressure."

My companion was even paler by now. He asked: "How did you know? I have been experiencing everything you mentioned but thought it was all in my head! I work 24/7, make lots of money, regret the time I don't spend with my young ones, I "live" on coffee during the day, I (shyly) drink at night so I can sleep, and I have also taken sleep medications... I have had a couple of those dreadful *waking-up in the middle of the night with chest-pain experiences*, dismissed them because I had no time to even go to the hospital... It was a dreadful experience. I thought I was alone..."

CHAPTER 1

LEADING UNDER PRESSURE

Working women and men currently face greater responsibilities than in the past. They have access to higher positions within their workplace, endlessly juggling tasks, and attempting to master productive and rewarding interactions. At the same time, they face increasing household duties. While some succeed in managing this complex act, others end up dreading the once-wonderful new opportunities. Burnt-out, energy-depleted, or miserably depressed, unable to enjoy their accumulated wealth, "having it all" yet unable to taste enjoyment, some executives find themselves working as an automaton, unable to take pleasure from their hard-earned position and financial stability.

Many of these workers feel that they are being cheated by the system of success. On the one hand they are giving their jobs the best of their lives – their energy and their passion – and yet they are profoundly ambivalent about being worn-out in their personal lives. Many feel deflated when they go home, facing a number of responsibilities waiting for them as they arrive, tired from an exhausting day. Instead of revitalizing, connecting with their loved ones, relaxing and enjoying life as they recharge their batteries for the next day, their time at home is just a continuation of a "busy day at work."

The increase in demands in the workplace and in the "homeplace" calls for the implementation of new lifestyle strategies to effectively succeed in long-term objectives, initiatives, and planning. Although some people may need to perform the same task every day, the entrepreneur or the corporate executive does both: she or he performs similar tasks every day and lives in constant change. A few would be able to sustain quality and top performance in a task that requires constant repetition. In our quantum-leaping reality, moving up or across the corporate ladder is a dominant factor that most executives face at any given time in their professional careers. Although many may choose lateral moves, they are still "moving" within their organizational structures. With this constant change, many executives leave behind some very basic needs as they are consumed with work. Executives do not have a choice other than to master the art of management and integration, demanded by the ever-changing, progressive corporate environmental demands.

The best athletes possess the biological ability to lower their metabolic needs to baseline levels during between-competition periods. This capability allows them to re-energize and increase their output during the next event, match, or game. Like athletes, corporate executives are likely to exert extraordinary outputs of stamina during their careers. Unlike athletes, though, executives do not have the luxury of sitting down and relaxing to bring their hyperactive metabolism to a resting state before going into another strenuous phase, as they tend to juggle multiple responsibilities at the same time. Top executives go on to resolve the next task even before they have completed the previous one. Top executives strive to anticipate the following task before there is a tangible need for it. At the same time, it is imperative for executives to be capable of creating temporary illusions of unwinding in such a way that their integrated persona may recuperate from exhausting work while still in action. Top executives should target the ability to work on multiple issues at different intensities and at the precise speed that each task requires.

Running a single sprint is a rare occurrence in the life of the globe-trotting corporate warrior. Over the course of their complex schedules, executives and professionals will most likely need to run two, three, or more sprints, at the same time, and keep going in the marathon. This poses a dilemma. As many feel like they are already at their maximum performance, is there any room for improvement? Is improvement unbounded or is there a limit to our capabilities? If executives feel like they have "maxed out," can they lead their team to achieve a higher goal? If so, what is the turn-key? What is that treasured strategy to do this, once, twice, and all over again?

As athletes strive to achieve Olympic records, expert physiologists wonder how much longer records will be broken without the "assistance" of stimulants and artificial performance enhancers... Year after year, athletes come closer and even surpass prior unbelievable achievements and unimaginable triumph.

High achievers with little tolerance for defeat leave themselves a narrow space to take a deep breath and relax before undertaking the next Herculean task. The pressure they put upon themselves to fulfill their dreams and achieve their projects is such that they project their deadlines and write these down on their calendars "To Be Completed: Yesterday." As they succeed, many devote little time to enjoy their accomplishment, as they are already into their next task, without savoring their well-deserved victory.

It is this group of executives or entrepreneurs that procrastinates in seeking advice or assistance, and it is this group that usually looks for help once signs and symptoms of obvious burn-out are present. As these executives realize there is a clear impact upon the overall quality of their work, they come to a state of disbelief. Their colleagues and friends may not notice this decrease in performance, as these high achievers usually perform at the top level and output of three people instead of one. While these outstanding achievers are in their twenties, they are able to push themselves to levels where only a selected few have ever reached. As these executives and entrepreneurs grow into their forties and fifties, their ability to bounce back ceases to be as effective as in the past. What could have gone wrong? As they try over and over again, they realize their unique, praised ability to do it all has left them for good.

Some of these successful executives and entrepreneurs would increasingly struggle with maintaining their healthy body weight, cholesterol levels, and blood pressure within normal ranges. They may now find difficulty with falling or staying asleep, they may struggle with body tension, and experience difficulty relaxing. They may gradually increase the consumption of caffeinated drinks during the day to "stay alert and awake," to continue to perform as they did in their twenties. They may decide to have an extra drink at night to fall asleep after an exhausting day. This harmful sequence of events is now in full force, creating a constant negative cycle, unless there is an intervention sooner rather than later. Unattended, the risks include the potential for increasing discomfort or disease. The initial symptoms may be vague, such as gastrointestinal complaints, anxiety, pain, or fatigue. In more extreme cases, chest pain, gastrointestinal ulcers, or full-blown panic attacks would bring these executives to the emergency room. Often times, they may have endured endless doubts about consulting a professional earlier on, in the hopes that this distress would magically disappear. Tormented with obsessional thoughts about whether or not there is a "physical" problem and how to seek help, dreading the stigma of being labeled as sick, anxious, depressed, or physically unfit in any shape or form, they resist any perceived danger of falling off from the hard-earned pedestal of invincibility as the super-powered, successful entrepreneur or executive.

I have consistently found that it is this group that truly benefits from implementing a comprehensive, proactive, and integrated approach. Your roadmap to wellbeing includes:

- **LEARN THE FACTS:** The first step is to know the facts. Identify the different elements within the Wellbeing & Stress continua. Identify your Pressure Points. Learn about stress, resilience, depression, and anxiety. Learn about how stress can impact upon your health.

- **ASSESS YOUR SITUATION:** The second step is to assess your individual and organizational health and wealth situation using the Four Quadrants of *Leading Under Pressure* and to align with the corresponding strategies.

- **IMPLEMENT EFFECTIVE STRATEGIES:** The third step is to implement effective strategies to maximize your health while building your wealth.

If you are *Leading Under Pressure*, it will be a question of time to decide when you are ready to master your life challenges and opportunities. Today is a great day to start: assess, fix, and plan ahead. As an executive or entrepreneur, you have dedicated a great part of your life to your career and business. With *Leading Under Pressure* you will address the first step of your journey. *Managing Work in Life* will go a step further in addressing the Physical, Emotional, Intellectual, Social, and Spiritual dimensions of individuals and organizations. Let's get started by providing the key elements to eventually create your own *New Life Business Plan* as you merge analyses and strategies into a comprehensive mode of action, combining individual, professional, and organizational needs and strategies in an effective, integrative, and long-lasting plan. *Quantum Wellbeing* is the culmination of the series with the broad implementation of *"The Four Pillars of Biological Health"*, putting it all together, practicing and mastering each and every dimension to the fullest.

CHAPTER 2

THE WELLBEING & STRESS CONTINUA

Stress can be a wonderful source of energy, motivation, and inspiration. However, if stress increases and our compensatory mechanisms are unable to react to escalating demands, since the system gives in, burnout, exhaustion, and eventually disease may develop.

The Wellbeing & Stress *continua* concept provides for a practical way to assess our degree of wellbeing. To my surprise, I have been encountering more and more people telling me the culprit for all their aches and pains is their enormous amount of stress, rather than realizing they are experiencing obvious signs and symptoms of illness and disease at a stage where stress just aggravates the situation but is not the cause.

Stigma has played a major role in entrepreneurs' and executives' ignoring their underlying physical ailments, including significant degrees of depression and anxiety. Telling the world they are stressed is expected; after all, they are "supposed" to be working incredibly long hours and competing at their top level. Instead of seeking help in a timely fashion, many are daring to visit their physician only when they are already experiencing more than one medical problem.

Whether executives face a crisis that acutely increases their stress level affecting their wellbeing or whether they encounter chronic stressors on a regular basis, or both (which may happen more often than the first two instances), executives must attempt to utilize this source of energy as an opportunity to address their needs and, once resolved, continue to improve their overall situation. Contrary to this, most attempt to go back to the previous situation, in a futile attempt to avoid inevitable change. My suggestion is not only to resolve the critical situation but to strategically plan ahead and continue to improve, advancing to a new level. A critical event may increase the level of stress and may acutely affect the person's continuous improvement to maximize wellbeing. Modern Western medicine has continuously attempted to "resolve" the problem and go back to the non-acute baseline. This strategy works well as long as the person has a healthy baseline. For instance, if a healthy individual has a bout of illness such as an infection, the right strategy may be to resolve the infection and to move on. On the other end, if the person's baseline is unhealthy (i.e.: the person is obese, with high blood pressure, and diabetic) and this person falls ill, the health strategy should, instead, focus on resolving the acute issue and attempting to pursue a healthier baseline rather than "patching" the situation with medications alone. Our culture craves quick fixes and immediate gratification rather than thoughtful planning and comprehensive interventions.

The Wellbeing & Stress continua are inversely related: the higher the level of stress, the less the degree of wellbeing. While someone can be under stress, he or she may still experience wellbeing. However, as pressure increases, the person may still be able to experience wellness up to a "point of no return," where compensatory systems start giving in and the energy system becomes exhausted. Please note each of us has an individual perception of stress: we interpret and respond to stressors in different ways.

The Wellbeing & Stress Continua

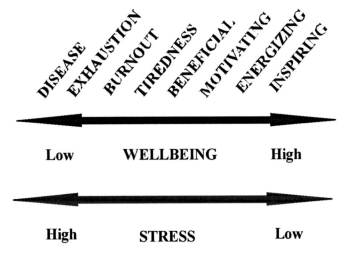

Figure 1: The Wellbeing & Stress Continua

CHAPTER 3

PRESSURE POINTS

WHAT IS STRESS?

Common to all definitions of stress is a focus on environmental conditions that threaten to impair the wellbeing of the individual. Stress may occur either as an acute event or as chronic difficulty, and as a major life event or as small events with cumulative effects (either added or multiplied). Stressful events may be within a normal age-related expectation, such as going to college or starting a job for the first time, or an extraordinary event such as being in an abusive situation, and may be related to or totally independent of the person's actions. The subjective threat of a stressor directly relates to the person's sensitivity toward an event as stressful and this perception will, in turn, impact the person's psychological wellbeing. There may be a high genetic predisposition to how each individual perceives and reacts to a stressful situation. Furthermore, some will be able to face some stressors without difficulty (i.e.: stressors at work) and the same person may have a harder time while encountering other stressors (i.e.: stressors as they relate to their relationships with family members). Finally, some specific stressors may be more highly related to depression and anxiety disorders than others.

There is scientific evidence to suggest a stressor may have a direct effect on the development of a first depressive episode but not on subsequent ones. This means that someone with a strong predisposition may develop a first episode of depression during or after a significant stressful event.

Eventually, the person may become depressed again, and, although people will try to justify the second episode and link it to another stressful event, there is little evidence to support this. On the contrary, by tracking the series of events, we can identify that the person may have gradually become more depressed and may have started to experience problems with their significant others and at work long before the full-blown depression was identified.

PRESSURE POINTS

Stress can be motivating, stimulating, inspiring, and an amazing source of energy. Given the subjective nature of the experience of stress, some of us will thrive under pressure whereas others will succumb to its powerful force. Some executives will wait to the last moment to submit proposals, finalize deals, negotiate opportunities, and execute plans, taking advantage of the biological adrenaline rush whereas others will pace themselves in finding a good balance in timing easier and more complex tasks. People's reaction to stress is very different.

Physical Pressure Points
- Fatigue and being overly tired
- Physical exhaustion
- Sleep deprivation
- Hunger
- Over-exercise

Emotional Pressure Points
- Conflict with spouse, children, or siblings
- Conflict with friends
- Conflict with colleagues
- Conflict with boss
- Conflict with clients

Intellectual Pressure Points
- Inability to keep up with work demands from an intellectual perspective
- Lack of time to study or prepare
- Intellectual exhaustion secondary to sleep deprivation

Social Pressure Points
- Isolation
- Lack of connectivity with others at home or at work
- Social mismatch between family of origin, friends, and/or work

Spiritual Dimension
- Mismatch between personal and organizational values
- Feeling like there is no reward after so much effort
- Inability to experience a deep spiritual connection with higher being

In 1967, Holmes and Rahe described the Social Readjustment Scale. The ten most significant stressful life events include:

1. Death of spouse
2. Divorce or separation
3. Marital separation from spouse
4. Legal proceedings or prison term
5. Death of a close family member
6. Major personal injury or illness
7. Marriage and parenthood
8. Being fired from a job
9. Marital reconciliation with a spouse
10. Retirement from work

Seven self-imposed pressure points that I most commonly see in my practices include:

- Responding to every need as if it was necessary and as if there was no choice to do it or not
- Trying to live up to others' expectations at all times
- Wanting to continue to move on to the next level to achieve more without taking a minute to enjoy the present success
- Feeling constantly dissatisfied: nothing is enough
- Constantly comparing and competing with others rather than competing with self
- Creating impossible deadlines that cannot be achieved by the desired time
- Disjointed priorities: the person says something is terribly important but his/her actions or behavior does not match the supposed sense of urgency

Stressful events don't necessarily need to be negative in nature, such as becoming a parent or having teenagers off to college. These, though, can be a tremendous source of stress. I have particularly seen this in business women who have their first child in their late thirties or early forties. Many continue strenuous exercise until their personal physician has to ask them to stop playing tennis, flying, or lifting heavy boxes during their eighth month of pregnancy. Many feel like they will go back to their full workload immediately after delivering their child. They soon find themselves in the dilemma of wanting to spend more time with their baby and having a highly demanding job. Pregnancy and parenting add an important source of stress both from an emotional as well as physical perspective.

STRATEGY: A simple strategy is to attempt to identify, pre-plan, and pace the activities and responsibilities that can be almost "automatically" carried on. Anticipate more demanding times and needs looking at your past experience, so that high performance and productivity will be maintained at all times.

It is essential for each to identify the sources of stress and the pressure points. What dimension is the one that triggers most of your challenges: physical stress, emotional, intellectual, social, or spiritual? Once you can identify the underlying dimension that is affected the most, it is easier to concentrate on fixing that one area by implementing effective strategies. This area is fully developed in **Managing Work in Life**.

CHAPTER 4

FACTS ABOUT ACUTE AND CHRONIC STRESS

ACUTE STRESS may provoke a series of signs and symptoms ranging from mild anxiety to an acute panic attack or a freezing reaction. However, prolonged, unrelieved exposure to a variety of stressors may cause a person to operate in a physiological "full-alert" mode at all times, as if a catastrophe was about to occur at any moment, thus operating in a hyper alert state.

Whether the outside stressor continues to exist or whether the person fails to return to his or her baseline level of functioning, it is essential for the person to create a state of mind of control. If the person continues to experience a stressor as constant, whether or not the stressor is actually present in the environment, the person runs the risk of failing to adapt to the same stressor over time, potentially exhausting individual strategies to bounce back and master the situation. If fatigue occurs, the ability of the individual's system to refuel itself gives in, and this is why many continue to operate under stress mode even if the stressor has disappeared: they do this because they are unable to re-energize their system.

While stress affects all dimensions of the human being, what may start as an experience within one area, such as the emotional dimension, will further impact upon other dimensions: physical, intellectual, social, and spiritual. Additionally, elevated levels of stress hormones for long periods of time may potentially impair memory as well. High cortisol levels may promote loss of nerve cells, further producing atrophy of key brain structures that may further affect future responses to stress. Neuroplasticity - the brain's ability to reorganize itself by forming more neural connections through life - becomes a key element for re-mastering and re-training ourselves to respond more positively to acute or chronic stress, thus modifying our chances of long-term difficulties.

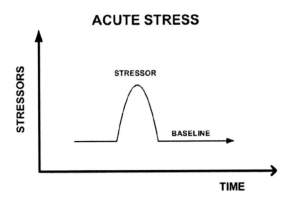

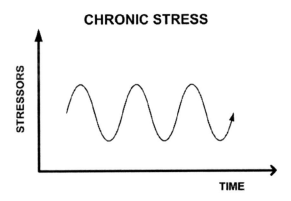

Figure 2: Acute & Chronic Stress

CHRONIC STRESS relates to continuous stress. Although not described in psychiatry, many people may be subjected to ongoing, constant stress rather than being exposed to a single traumatic event. This could be described as a **Constant Traumatic Stress syndrome**, where the person is exposed to both acute events as well as constant stressors of different magnitudes. An example of this would be people living in countries at war, both as civilians or as military personnel. Also, those operating under extreme circumstances where there is ongoing violence while business is "operating as usual" may be subjected to chronic stress as well. More studies to differentiate the physiology of those exposed to a single traumatic event versus ongoing stressors need to be in place to further define each subgroup correctly.

Corporate executives and entrepreneurs face both acute and chronic stress on a regular basis: acute instances of stress (i.e.: a specific deadline such as the opening of a new facility or the launch of a new product) as well as dealing with ongoing, "chronic" levels of stress (i.e. third downsizing in three years). An example of both would be executives in charge of an operation in countries with increased ongoing violence facing individual security problems on a regular basis.

STRATEGY: The overall strategy in this situation is to control the chronic stressors as much as possible, and to be ready to intervene with the more acute or more severe stressors.

TYPES OF CHRONIC STRESS

- **Periodic Stressors:** are similar stressors that occur on a regular basis: such as monthly reports.

- **Occasional Stressors:** are unanticipated stressors of different magnitude. The person may go back to baseline between stressors.

- **Cumulative Stressors:** are unanticipated stressors of different magnitude that do not allow the person to go back to baseline and recover.

Entrepreneurs and executives most commonly experience multiple stressors of different magnitude at the same time and at different times.

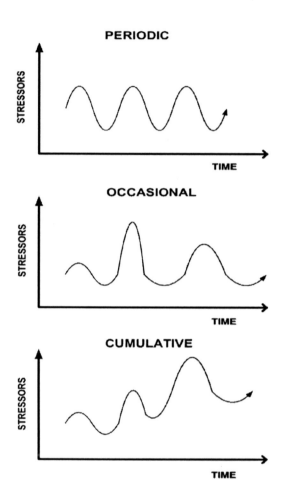

Figure 3: Types of Chronic Stressors

CHAPTER 5

THE STRESS RESPONSE
& RESILIENCE

As described earlier, stress relates to the absolute magnitude of the stressor and the person's perception of the stressor. The Fight-or-Flight-or-Freeze response interferes with high-level intellectual functioning and basically affects each and every dimension.

SIGNS OF STRESS ACROSS DIMENSIONS

Physical Signs of Stress:
- Fatigue
- Dizziness
- Headaches
- Sweating
- Gastro-intestinal problems
- Heart palpitations
- Increase in the startle reflex
- Tremors
- Colds
- Vague pains and aches
- Change in sleep
- Change in diet

Emotional Signs of Stress
- Fear
- Terror
- Anger
- Guilt
- Anxiety

- Frequent crying
- Irritability
- Inappropriate humor
- Decreased interest in pleasurable activities
- Emotional exhaustion or feeling overwhelmed
- Emotional outbursts

Intellectual Signs of Stress
- Reduced attention span
- Decreased concentration
- Calculation difficulties
- Memory problems
- Decision-making difficulties
- Confusion

Social Signs of Stress
- Social withdrawal
- Isolation
- Increased substance use

Spiritual Signs of Stress
- Questioning values and beliefs
- Constant cynicism
- Loss of meaning or purpose
- Directing anger toward God
- Helplessness
- Hopelessness

Longer Term Effects of Stress include:
- Problems at work
- Problems in school
- Problems at home, with spouse, and children
- Relationship problems with family members, friends, and colleagues
- Medical problems including depression and anxiety

WHAT IS RESILIENCE?

Resilience is the ability to positively adapt in the face of adversity. Our perception of stressful factors and our tool box to respond to extreme sources of distress will be key components to our response to adversity, and it will be measured by our ability to bounce back. People commonly demonstrate different levels of resilience. Our resilience is a combination of our own genetic background, our environmental exposure to different challenges, and our learned behavior to respond. Resilience is an active process that you may enhance. Please note most people strive to go back to their "normal" baseline after facing challenges. The truth is that the reality that once existed no longer does. You may want to "create" the illusion that you have gone back to baseline. Bouncing back may provide for an excellent opportunity for growth, moving on to the next phase.

Every time we succeed in coping effectively with a difficult situation, we are actually "priming" ourselves in dealing with subsequent stressful situations that may be beyond our control. The brain circuitry that "controls" our ability to bounce back includes brain areas such as the prefrontal cortex and the dorsal raphe nucleus in the brainstem. In general, I have observed that when we are able to succeed even in tough situations, when re-exposed to another stressor, we may be more able to respond in a successful way rather than if we had not been able to succeed the first time. One thing leads to another; this is why it is so important to enable positive experiences so as to continue to improve. This concept justifies allowing ourselves to savor and experience success in the "here and now" before moving ahead to the next challenge. Another common example is public speaking. If we leave the stage with a full blown panic attack, we will be more likely to have increased anticipatory anxiety if exposed to a similar situation in the future. In contrast, if the person is able to deliver the talk in spite of the initial tension, this will enable the individual set up his or her own "stage of mind" to perform well the next time.

Resilience is an area which also relates to our ability to live up to the occasion in a critical situation. There are no tests that measure who will be able to successfully react to a stressful situation in contrast with someone else. Someone who may have been trained for extreme situations may become "paralyzed" during an acute event whereas someone who seems to panic with everyday-life issues may be able to "play it cool" and take charge in a catastrophic event.

STRATEGY: Look back in time and identify how well you responded during stressful times. If you are working with a team, analyze how others responded during stressful times and identify their talents. Consider organizing and planning a group of intervention with pre-assigned tasks in case of an emergency situation. Role-play, test your plan, and continue to improve the response.

CHAPTER 6

MEDICAL ILLNESSES WITH A STRESS COMPONENT

Albert is a CEO in his late fifties. He has been a successful family man and leader of a large financial organization for years. For the past decade, he has experienced increasing pressure at work, as more competing companies have come to existence and disappeared. His adult children are caring for themselves, yet Albert feels like he carries a world of responsibilities on his back: although he intellectually understands his role, he feels responsible for every person within his organization and believes nothing works well unless he is there to handle it all. Albert is a self-made man, trained in the traditional style: a company owner needs to be involved from A to Z within his organization. His managers and employees firmly believe he micromanages everyone at work and he will often call work during family time or vacation (that is, if he takes vacation at all.) Albert believes the world will fall apart unless he is everywhere. He has been visiting his family physician more often in the recent months. His doctor has told him how stressful events have impacted upon his health, leading to episodes of high blood pressure and gastrointestinal problems. In spite of his doctor's recommendations, Albert stopped exercising after an unanticipated financial loss, feeling he had to dedicate more time to work. He has experienced severe headaches which were linked to high blood pressure episodes, now treated with medications. Additionally, he has been experiencing gastrointestinal upset for years, and has been restricting his diet more and more as he has now become intolerant to certain foods. He has difficulty sleeping and feels drained and grumpy most days. His hectic schedule doesn't help: Albert travels coast-to-coast, across meridians around the globe, accommodating to time changes, cultures, and nutritional styles.

THE STRESS RESPONSE

Increasing levels of stress may affect individuals to different degrees. Those who may already be suffering conditions such as diabetes or hypertension may experience worsening of their condition during times of increased stress.

Stress may have a direct impact on each and every system; Central Nervous System: increasing tension and migraine headaches, or triggering a first episode of depression or anxiety, or both. It may affect the endocrine system by destabilizing the person's thyroid function or worsening diabetes. Stress may impact the cardiovascular system by increasing the potential for angina or increasing the probability of having a heart attack. Stress may contribute to triggering an asthma attack, directly impacting upon the pulmonary system, an ulcer via the gastrointestinal system, and so on.

It is essential to understand the differences between stress, depression, and anxiety disorders, as the appropriate intervention for each varies. Unfortunately, many individuals may not recognize their symptoms as signs of an illness, or they may fear the reactions of colleagues, friends, and family. As a result, millions of people with depression or anxiety do not seek treatment. Instead, they experience problems at their jobs and in their relationships which could have been avoided if addressed earlier.

In summary, the following are some medical illnesses with a Stress component:

MEDICAL ILLNESSES WITH A STRESS COMPONENT

Neurological and Psychiatric Disorders
- Tension and Migraine Headaches
- Stroke
- Pain
- Depression
- Anxiety

Endocrine Disorders
- Diabetes
- Hypo or Hyperthyroidism
- Adrenal-related conditions

Cardiovascular and Pulmonary Disorders
- Asthma
- Hypertension
- Angina Pectoris
- Myocardial Infarction

Gastro-Intestinal Disorders
- Colitis
- Gastric Ulcers
- Irritable Bowel Syndrome

CHAPTER 7

FACTS ABOUT DEPRESSION

Larry has been a successful entrepreneur, caring for his family business for years. In his early thirties, he experienced a time of low energy. Everything seemed to be going well in his business, but he lacked the push to perform at his highest level. His family and friends became concerned because he was always perceived as an overachiever, enjoying his successes. Larry had always been athletic and always took good care of his health. At the time, he was unable to sleep well at night, waking up hours before his regular waking time, unable to go back to sleep. His appetite drastically decreased and he lost weight, prompting others to alarm. Larry felt the world had lost its beautiful colors and music had lost its harmony. He felt nothing inspired him to continue his daily existence. His wife became alarmed when he missed going to work - which was out of character for him - and she consulted his family. Larry's father suggested he visit their family doctor, as he realized many of the signs and symptoms his son was showing were similar to the ones he had also experienced decades earlier. Larry had a full work-up and other medical conditions were ruled-out. Larry was educated about depression and a successful intervention was implemented. Since then, Larry has effectively dealt with depression. He can identify early signs and symptoms of depression and intervene as soon as possible.

Depression is a serious medical illness that negatively affects your thoughts, your feelings, your behavior, your ability to communicate with others, and thus your ability to connect with your loved ones. To receive a diagnosis of clinical depressive disorder, signs and symptoms of depression would be severe enough to impact upon your functioning at work and at home. Depression is a common illness that affects close to twenty million Americans across gender, age, race, ethnicity, and socioeconomic status every year. Although depression can strike at any time, it most often appears for the first time between the mid-twenties to mid-forties. Women experience depression twice as often as men in their lifetime.

The costs of depression are high, affecting individuals, their families, and organizations. The estimated financial costs of depression in missed days at work, medical expenses, and premature death are $43 billion annually in the United States. Üstün et al described depression as the fourth leading cause of disease burden worldwide, accounting for 4.4% of total DALYs – Disability Adjusted Life Years - in the year 2000.

Feelings of sadness are expected to arise upon the death of a loved one, the loss of a job, or the ending of a relationship. In the normal process of sadness, feelings of sadness will decrease with time. Instead, clinical depression can continue for months or years if left to its natural course.

Depression includes a variety of symptoms, but one of these two elements must be present to make the diagnosis:

1. A persistent feeling of sadness or
2. The loss of interest or pleasure in usual activities. Either one or both symptoms must be present most days for a period of two weeks to consider depression as a potential diagnosis. Additionally, the person must experience four or more of the following

symptoms to make a diagnosis of depression:

3. Changes in appetite that result in weight loss or gain (not related to dieting)
4. Insomnia or oversleeping
5. Loss of energy or increased fatigue or tiredness
6. Restlessness or irritability
7. Feelings of worthlessness or inappropriate guilt
8. Difficulty thinking, concentrating, or making decisions
9. Thoughts of death or suicide or attempts at suicide

Depression is diagnosed only if the above symptoms are not due to other medical conditions or if they are not the unexpected side effects of medications or substance abuse.

Diagnostic and Statistical Manual of Mental Disorders, American Psychiatric Association.

SIGNS & SYMPTOMS OF DEPRESSIVE DISORDERS

Physical Signs and Symptoms of Depression
- Sleep Disturbances
- Appetite change with weight change
- Loss of energy
- Agitation or slowness
- Decreased libido
- Physical complaints
- Vague pains and aches, including headaches and abdominal pain

Emotional Signs and Symptoms of Depression
- Anxiety
- Lack of pleasure
- Melancholia
- Depressed or sad mood
- Irritable or cranky mood: "moody"

Intellectual Signs and Symptoms of Depression
- Difficulty concentrating
- Feelings of worthlessness
- Sense of guilt
- Low self-esteem
- Negative image of self
- Disorganized thinking or presence of psychosis

Social Signs and Symptoms of Depression
- Social isolation or withdrawal
- Easily angered or agitated
- Change in normal way of interacting with others

Spiritual Signs and Symptoms of Depression
- Loss of interest in daily activities

- Feelings of hopelessness and helplessness
- Suicidal thoughts, acts or attempts
- Question of values
- Negative outlook of future

If you believe you may have clinical depression, consult your personal physician or a psychiatrist. Depression is one of the most treatable medical conditions, and, with proper treatment, individuals can regain their health and continue to enjoy their outlook on life.

CHAPTER 8

FACTS ABOUT ANXIETY

A lex has always been looked up to and has been considered very successful in all her business endeavors. She has had a recent promotion into a job that is quite demanding, requiring skills she does not feel she has mastered. She experiences daily discomfort, feeling she will be "found out," although her performance and productivity have been excellent. She has always been good thinking "on her feet." She is suddenly asked to give a presentation to upper management without prior preparation. A colleague minimizes the depth the presentation requires and she finds herself in front of unknown, serious faces, "staring" at her without prior introduction. As she looks around, Alex feels that her heart is about to explode out of her chest, her palms are soaking wet, and she is breathing fast. She blanks her introduction, mumbling shyly and in a disorganized manner. The first few minutes were torture but she eventually managed to overcome the unpleasant situation and bounce back. She still does not remember what she was thinking or saying those first few minutes, but the symptoms she experienced are still fresh in her mind and she fears they will come back.

Anticipating a tough business deal, having an important job interview, or giving a presentation to a tough audience, may be good reasons for feeling a little anxious. Sweaty palms and "butterflies" in the stomach during challenging situations are not uncommon. However, normal feelings of nervousness differ significantly from anxiety disorders, another very treatable medical condition. An anxiety attack often occurs unexpectedly, impacting upon the daily routine in an unprecedented way. Anxiety disorders are the most common of emotional disorders, annually affecting more than 20 million Americans.

While people may try to connect their feelings of nervousness in response to an event and these feelings may go away after the event has passed; instead, anxiety disorders often occur for no apparent reason and repeat over time. When anxiety disorders are present, the person reacts as if she or he were in a state of alarm to which the person needs to constantly decide to fight or flee. This exhausting mechanism further burns out the individual, as she or he anticipates the next attack. These alarming reactions can make everyday experiences sources of dread. If left untreated, job performance, work productivity, and personal relationships inevitably suffer as a result.

Much like in depression, anxiety disorders generally respond well to treatment and the majority of patients receiving treatment experience significant relief from their symptoms. Unfortunately, many people with anxiety disorders do not seek treatment because they do not recognize their symptoms as a sign of illness or they fear the reactions of colleagues, family, or friends. More so, many state they are burnt-out or exhausted when they are actually experiencing full-blown panic attacks.

TYPES OF ANXIETY DISORDERS

Panic Disorder, Phobias, Obsessive-Compulsive Disorder, Post Traumatic Stress Disorder, and Generalized Anxiety Disorders are included in this category. I would like to comment on both Panic Disorders and Post Traumatic Stress Disorders, as I believe these may both be the most significant in relationship to the stress continuum and on how these affect the lives of busy executives who are Leading Under Pressure.

Panic Disorder

The key symptom of panic disorder is the panic attack, an overwhelming fear of being in danger or about to die, during which the individual may experience mostly physical, emotional, and intellectual symptoms, including:

Physical Signs and Symptoms of Panic Disorder
- Pounding heart or chest pain
- Sweating, trembling, or shaking
- Shortness of breath or sensation of choking
- Nausea or abdominal pain
- Dizziness or lightheadedness
- Chills or hot flashes

Emotional Signs and Symptoms of Panic Disorder
- Numbness
- Fear of losing control, "going crazy," or dying

Intellectual Signs and Symptoms of Panic Disorder
- Feeling of impending doom
- Feeling unreal or disconnected

Social Signs and Symptoms of Panic Disorder
- Avoidance of frequenting places that "remind" of the event or place where the first episode took place
- Isolation

Spiritual Signs and Symptoms of Panic Disorder
- Hopelessness
- Fear of death
- Helplessness

Because these attacks occur unexpectedly and seemingly without reason, people with panic disorder often first believe that they are having a heart attack. One of the most challenging issues around Panic Disorder is convincing the person who has been experiencing the attacks to shift their conviction that there is an underlying physical problem to a psychological one. Panic attacks have manifestations across dimensions and it is important to address the underlying cause so that people can be effectively treated.

Posttraumatic Stress Disorder

Posttraumatic stress disorder (PTSD) occurs in individuals who have experienced, witnessed, or survived a severe or terrifying event. People with PTSD keep re-experiencing the ordeal 24/7 through memories of the events during waking hours and recurrent nightmares during sleep. They experience flashbacks as well as extreme physical, emotional, intellectual, social, and spiritual distress when exposed to situations that remind them of the traumatic event.

Events that can trigger PTSD include witnessing or experiencing military combat, violent personal attacks, man-made or natural disasters, and physical or sexual abuse.

As in depression, genetic, environmental, and stress factors may contribute to the onset of anxiety disorders.

CHAPTER 9

MEDICAL INTERVENTIONS FOR DEPRESSION AND ANXIETY DISORDERS

If you believe you may be experiencing depression or anxiety, consult your personal physician or request an evaluation by a psychiatrist. Depression and Anxiety disorders are two of the most treatable medical conditions, and, with proper treatment, individuals can regain their wellbeing.

A comprehensive assessment is key. Although medication treatment can be very effective for the treatment of depression or anxiety, or both, I have found that it is very important to guide patients in committing to make integrative approaches to improve each and every aspect of their lives. My approach as a psychiatrist is to offer intensive, integrative, and comprehensive interventions with a holistic approach. My own commitment has always been to assist my patients to not only overcome their episode of depression or anxiety, but to truly aspire to improve toward achieving their best and to enjoy fulfilling lives. This is a major contrast with most of what the current US healthcare system offers in a few minutes of evaluation or follow-up treatment. As a business coach, I would continue to work on prioritizing strategies and organizational skills, referring the person to have an appropriate evaluation by a family physician or psychiatrist.

The length of treatment or proper combination of interventions is determined on a case-by-case basis, meaning that treatment depends on each individual person. For example, someone experiencing a first mild episode of depression triggered by a catastrophic event with an excellent support system and a healthy history may benefit from being monitored for six months to a year. On the other end, someone experiencing a third episode of severe depression with a strong family history of depression may need to be followed for years.

An effective approach to treat depression and anxiety includes one or a combination of the following interventions:

PSYCHOTHERAPY

The following psychotherapy styles have been proven effective in the treatment of depression and anxiety disorders: Supportive Therapy, Cognitive-Behavioral Therapy (CBT), Intensive Brief Dynamic Psychotherapy, and Psycho-education. Self-help books may provide a combined educational and CBT perspective. Please note that Cognitive-Behavioral Therapy is the basis for coaching.

PSYCHOPHARMACOLOGY

Psychopharmacology is an effective biological treatment for moderate to severe cases of depression or anxiety. One or a combination of medications may be needed. These medications include: Selective Reuptake Inhibitors such as fluoxetine, sertraline, paroxetine, and escitalopram among others; Atypical antidepressants such as venlafaxine, bupropion (also approved for the use of smoking cessation), and duloxetine (also approved for neuropathic pain); Monoamine Oxidase Inhibitors (for treatment-resistant depression), and anxiolytics. The use of herbals such as St. John's Wort may be useful in mild to moderate cases of depression, and there is some evidence of the positive effects of Omega 3 Fatty Acids as adjunctive use in combination with FDA approved antidepressants. Acupuncture and other naturopathic interventions may add value to the regimen. More research is required in these other areas.

LIFESTYLE STRATEGIES

These interventions have become "complementary" in the Western world, when, in fact, they are an integral part of any medical intervention. These include what I call **"The Four Pillars of Biological Health:"** adequate nutrition, good sleep hygiene, regular exercise, and the practice of relaxation techniques on a regular basis. For a summary of **"The Four Pillars of Biological Health"** please read chapter 12, further described in **Managing Work in Life** and fully developed in the **Quantum Wellbeing** series.

For more information about depression and anxiety disorders, please visit the following websites:

- **WORLD HEALTH ORGANIZATION:**
  www.who.int/en/

- **NATIONAL INSTITUTE OF MENTAL HEALTH:** www.nimh.nih.gov

- **MENTAL HEALTH INFOSOURCE:**
  mhsource.com

- **AMERICAN PSYCHIATRIC ASSOCIATION:**
  www.HealthyMinds.org

- **NATIONAL DEPRESSION SCREENING DAY:**
  www.MentalHealthScreening.org

- AMERICAN PSYCHOLOGICAL ASSOCIATION: www.apa.org

- MEDSCAPE: www.medscape.com

- WEBMD: www.webmd.com

MEDICAL INTERVENTIONS FOR DEPRESSION AND ANXIETY DISORDERS

PSYCHOTHERAPY
(One or a combination)
- Supportive
- CBT
- Intensive Brief Dynamic Psychotherapy
- Psycho-Education

PSYCHOPHARMACOLOGY
(One or a combination)
- Selective Serotonin Reuptake Inhibitors (SSRIs)
- Atypical Antidepressants
- Monoamine Oxidase Inhibitors (MAOIs)
- Anxiolytics
- Herbals (consult for combinations)
- Complementary interventions

LIFESTYLE STRATEGIES: The Four Pillars of Biological Health
- Sleep
- Nutrition
- Exercise
- Relaxation

CHAPTER 10

FACTS ABOUT PERFORMANCE AND PRODUCTIVITY

PERFORMANCE reflects both an active process (how things get done and how long it takes for them to get done) and outcome (quality of the product and productivity). As an effective leader, you must operate on two paths simultaneously: the performance path with productivity as the final destination, and the people path, overseeing your employees' health, as described by Dr. Len Sperry in Effective Leadership. Being effective as a leader involves your expertise in both – for yourself, for your team, and for your organization.

The performance process is a dynamic development. As an active, fluid process, it presents the outstanding opportunity of constant improvement. At work, your performance evaluation includes the examination of the degree of knowledge, skills, abilities, quantity and quality of work, attitude toward work, communication skills with others as well as your level of initiative, degree of cooperation, dependability, judgment, leadership, organization, and planning abilities.

An adequate performance assessment system in business may include several components and should serve the purpose of overall and ultimate improvement. This purpose is fulfilled by having a feedback system in place, and will provide a tool and basis for salary increases and promotion, and overall direction of an employee's work.

This opportunity will also enable you identify specific areas for further training or improvement of skills for further development.

PRODUCTIVITY is a measure of outcomes and is the relationship of input to output. As productivity increases, profits increase as well as competitiveness in business or market share.

Based on the type of operation you and your business are involved in and what you are producing, you should choose a convenient measure of productivity. Measuring this dimension also includes a time frame in which you measure it.

Productivity will mean something different to each business whether it produces tangible products or services. The standard measurement of productivity is output per worker-hour, or the ratio between the number of hours-worked to the total output. You can also measure your productivity per week, month, or year, if each unit of production takes more than an hour to create. Output can be measured in terms of: volume, quantity of items produced, and the dollar value of the items produced.

It may be easier to measure your level of productivity if you concentrate, specifically, on your "produced output" at work. Based on our individual skills and capabilities, our training, studies, and experience, many of us may produce a proportional equivalent of the input we have invested. Some produce more and others produce less. For example, if I have had twelve years of studying and training for the sake of learning and then decide not to work or to work in an area completely different to the one in which I trained, some would argue the output produced in another area may not correspond with the input of trained years. On the other hand, if I am able to actively produce in accordance to the amount of invested training, the alignment may be perfect. Aligning the input with the product output is essential as an efficient use of energy.

CHAPTER II

INDIVIDUAL HEALTH & WEALTH ASSESSMENT & STRATEGIES

Consider the following as you further assess your individual health and your own level of performance and productivity (P2) as potential for wealth. Picture the x axis as one that describes your health, a continuous line going from little health to a state of total health and wellbeing. On the y axis, consider performance and productivity as your ability to transform your unique mix that makes you yourself as you apply your abilities and capabilities into a tangible output, your own ability to produce wealth. Although performance and productivity don't necessarily go "exactly" together, this exercise will allow you to assess your current situation and to then implement effective strategies to improve your situation. Please note, you may produce your wealth by an exchange of your work for money, as in a salary, or you may produce your wealth via the creation of your own company or investments.

I have repeatedly observed individuals (and organizations) implementing unaligned strategies: if the assessment is equivocal, the intervention will not match the need. Making the right assessment is essential prior to implementing the appropriate intervention.

The next section describes each quadrant for the individual and proposes effective strategies of intervention. Next, I will introduce a similar approach looking at the healthy and wealthy organization. I describe additional concepts in *Managing Work in Life*.

LEADING UNDER PRESSURE
The Quadrants

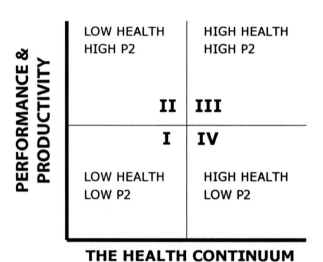

Figure 4: Leading Under Pressure: The Quadrants

QUADRANT I: LOW HEALTH, LOW P2

FOR THE INDIVIDUAL:

Mary is in her late fifties. She is widowed and has struggled with problems with her own health for some years and with her finances more recently. She has arthritis, moderate levels of recurring depression, and vague aches and pains described by the physician as fibromyalgia. When Mary's husband was alive, she was a housewife, bringing up her three now-grown children, who are currently all professionals. Although she has some savings and money available from her late husband's retirement, Mary faced the need to take a job to pay the bills, as she takes pride on being financially independent. Although she had studied years ago and was good at managerial jobs, she last worked decades ago, and is not familiar with the latest in computer use. Although her work ethics are impeccable, she comes to work on time and she tries to do well at work, Mary has trouble keeping up with the amount of work and the quality of her work, although good in effort, fails to accomplish the expectations as there always seems to be something missing...

ASSESSMENT: People in this category may be both acutely or chronically ill, affecting the individual's performance and productive capacity and, potentially, impacting upon wealth. Even if the person is wealthy, many resources will need to be allocated toward health-related issues, further impacting upon future wealth. This sector includes untreated medical conditions. One clear example in this area relates to obesity-related medical problems, including diabetes and hypertension. Any attempt to lower blood pressure and glucose levels without implementing strategies to improve nutrition and exercise will be futile. Currently, having surgery to reduce stomach capacity is en vogue (bariatric surgery). Although this surgery may help the person lose weight, bariatric surgery will not address the underlying, longstanding psychological and behavioral components that have enabled the person to put on tens or hundreds of pounds. Many people in this quadrant are in the process of becoming disabled or on disability. This quadrant includes increased levels of absenteeism (people being absent from work) and presenteeism (people being present at work but unable to perform).

STRATEGIES: Prioritizing your health needs to be improved upon first. It may feel overwhelming to attempt to fix what may seem to be many problems. Working on restoring health needs to be a priority. Next, coach and implement development skills in specific job areas after the health-related issues have improved.

I LOW HEALTH-
LOW P2

ASSESSMENT:

Acutely or chronically ill
Untreated medical conditions

Low Performance and
Productivity, low Wealth

STRATEGIES:

Improve Health first

Coach and Development Skills
Training next

Figure 5: Individual: QI: Low Health, Low
Productivity and Performance

QUADRANT II: LOW HEALTH, HIGH P2

FOR THE INDIVIDUAL:

Mark is in his fifties. As CEO of his own company, he has always worked like three people instead of one, and he has always bragged about this ability of his. He was always able to manage many challenges. Over the past few years, though, he has noticed an increase in his responsibilities and, although full of energy, he's also noticed he tires more easily. He has increased his coffee intake throughout the day to pump up his energy to be able to produce at the very high level he's usually produced. He has gradually increased his hours to sixteen working hours and will sometimes extend his waking hours to meet incredible deadlines. Although he was an athlete in his high school and college years, his lifestyle has become more sedentary with occasional brisk, sports-related activities with business colleagues. Although drinking socially has always been a part of his business activities, lately, he has also felt the need to increase his glass of wine to two or three accompanied by hard drinks at night to "relax" and sleep better. Some failed business and family stressors have added to his daily responsibilities. He has recently experienced more tension dealing with ongoing personal and business relationships, and some see him as being moody while his family describes him as cranky. Mark has recently experienced a couple of events where he woke up sweaty at night, heart pumping fast, perspiring profusely. He refused to go to the emergency room, as he is a strong believer he can deal with anything on his own...

ASSESSMENT: In this area, the individual is acutely or chronically ill (mild to severe). This area includes untreated medical conditions or ongoing uncompensated stress. In spite of being ill, the individual is still performing and producing at a high level. In the past, this individual may have worked like two, three, or four individuals, and only she or he may have noticed the decrease in performance or productivity. This is where many may have experienced burnout and energy depletion, subsequently experiencing more profound difficulties including panic attacks, depression or other stress-related medical conditions. This group has fallen into the negative cycle of using stimulants during the course of the day (both culturally accepted, prescribed, or illegal use of drugs) and hypnotics at night to maintain performance and productivity at the highest possible level.

STRATEGIES: Prioritize your health improvement process, put yourself first on your list beyond the "to do" list. If the health component continues to deteriorate, the person's health rapidly plummets into Quadrant I. Maximize your "Four Pillars of Biological Health." Manage stress. Avoid caffeine and alcohol in excess. Avoid too many caffeinated drinks and, if you smoke, stop smoking.

II LOW HEALTH - HIGH P2

ASSESSMENT:

Acutely or chronically ill
Untreated medical conditions

High Performance and
Productivity, High Wealth

STRATEGIES:

Improve Health. Evaluate and
treat underlying condition

Manage stress. Avoid caffeine
and alcohol in excess. Improve
The Four Pillars of Health

Figure 6: Individual: QII: Low Health, High
Productivity and Performance

QUADRANT III: HIGH HEALTH, HIGH P2

FOR THE INDIVIDUAL:

Max is a professional businesswoman in her forties. She has effectively juggled personal and professional responsibilities, leading a successful business and enjoying her family. She has experienced times in which she was able to produce at a high level and experienced extreme stress at the job, and other times, particularly when she felt a novice in a new job, where she was ready to start but lacked the preparation to succeed. She is now able to self-regulate her personal and professional needs and wants, and feels comfortable in prioritizing needs on a personal as well as on a professional level. She has learned to nicely say "no" along the way, and, although many people see her very involved with multiple activities, she strongly believes she has an ultimate plan that puts it all together. Max incorporates changes and new challenges one at a time: once she has been able to Improve, Achieve, and Maintain her desired goal, she can move on to her next level. She experiences joy in her personal life and in her work, as she believes she does what she was meant to do.

ASSESSMENT: In this quadrant, the individual is healthy or has medical issues under control. The individual maintains a high level of performance and productivity.

STRATEGIES: Identify the healthy strategies and continue to use them to continue your health and wealth situation. Establish specific goals to continue to improve within each and every area. Maximize **"The Four Pillars of Biological Health"** and challenge yourself along the way. If implementing new things, do this by bringing in one at a time. Improve, Achieve, and Maintain are core elements of **AIM IAM**, a system of constant improvement: *Align, Integrate, and Manage your Plan* while *Improving, Achieving, and Maintaining your Goals, described in depth in Managing Work in Life.*

III HIGH HEALTH- HIGH P2

ASSESSMENT:

Healthy or doing well under medical control. High Productivity and Performance

STRATEGIES:

Identify and continue to use successful strategies for Health and Wealth. Establish goals to continue to improve in each and every area Exercise/Nutrition/Sleep/Relax

Figure 7: Individual: QIII: High Health, High Productivity and performance

QUADRANT IV: HIGH HEALTH, LOW P2

FOR THE INDIVIDUAL:

Steph was a stellar worker on the technical end: well-respected, dependable, and a great colleague to others within her same group. Management liked her for her reliability and her agreeable disposition, as she used to comply with whatever was asked from her. When a more senior colleague stepped down as a manager, Steph was appointed by upper management to fill the vacant position. Although it was evident Steph struggled to continue with her technical responsibilities as well as her newly acquired administrative and managerial responsibilities, management believed it was just a matter of time for her to get used to managing it all. They assumed she would learn her new responsibilities as she "practiced" on the job and would "tell her" what to do and assumed she would understand how to do the job without further coaching. By the third and fourth month, Steph's work began to fail at every level. Not only did she struggle in managing others at work but also in completing her own work. Management began to express frustration with Steph and hardly realized it was they who had set up the young, pleasant, and driven employee for failure...

ASSESSMENT: In this quadrant, the individual is healthy or has medical issues under control. The individual either does not perform or produce, or performs poorly. This may be a young and/or new employee and/or an employee that may not have been placed in the best suited position at the job.

STRATEGIES: Identify the healthy strategies and continue to use them. The individual in this quadrant should seek for development and performance skills training. Consider increasing your knowledge by furthering training or education, seeking someone's coaching or mentoring, or career counseling. Establish specific goals to improve your situation. Maximize **"The Four Pillars of Biological Health"** and challenge yourself along the way.

IV HIGH HEALTH- LOW P2

ASSESSMENT:

Healthy but performing poorly

STRATEGIES:

Identify and continue to use successful strategies for Health.

Exercise/Nutrition/Sleep/Relax Development and Performance Skills Training. Further Education. Establish a plan for improvement

Figure 8: Individual: QIV: High Health, Low Productivity and Performance

IN SUMMARY: INDIVIDUAL HEALTH & WEALTH STRATEGIES:

If you find yourself in:

QUADRANT I: LOW HEALTH & LOW P2

Implement medical strategies first to improve your lifestyle and health, and then implement business strategies next.

QUADRANT II: LOW HEALTH & HIGH P2

Implement medical strategies first to improve your lifestyle and health. Make these a priority.

QUADRANT III: HIGH HEALTH & HIGH P2

Identify the healthy strategies and continue to use them to continue your health and wealth situation. Establish specific goals to continue to improve within each and every area.

QUADRANT IV: HIGH HEALTH & LOW P2

Identify the healthy strategies and continue to implement them. Maximize your development and performance skills training. Consider seeking further training or education, seek for a coach or mentor, and consider career counseling.

LEADING UNDER PRESSURE
Individual Strategies

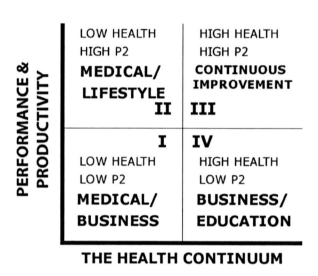

THE HEALTH CONTINUUM

Figure 9: Individual: Leading Under Pressure: Strategies

CHAPTER 12

ORGANIZATIONAL HEALTH & WEALTH ASSESSMENT & STRATEGIES

QUADRANT I: LOW HEALTH, LOW P2

FOR THE ORGANIZATION:

A *State-owned, non-profit organization has recently been privatized. Although processes and procedures are in place, the merging culture is misaligned: work styles are incompatible, the sense is chaotic, and there is an underlying animosity impacting upon employee morale affecting performance and productivity. The old and the new cultures clash: some say the old culture was better, whereas newly hired employees are determined to set up the tone with the new one. The new leadership comes in strong. However, it tries to force the new mode without facilitating the transition. Employee dissatisfaction leads to turnover, with massive exodus of "the best and the worst..."*

ASSESSMENT: Similarly to individuals, organizations in this category may be both acutely or chronically distressed, affecting organizational performance and productive capacity, impacting upon wealth. For example, an organization may have gone through a critical period losing its most valuable workers, keeping the ones who were reluctant to leave but who may be indifferent to the job. Even if the organization is wealthy, many resources will need to be allocated toward improving organizational health. This will, in turn, impact upon future wealth.

This organization may be experiencing high turnover and dissatisfaction in the workplace. It may also experience high indices of absenteeism and chaos, without proper leadership or a clear goal for everyone involved.

STRATEGIES: Improve the organization's health first. Identify the areas with the most challenges first, such as company structure and culture. Make it a priority to inspire and motivate employees to work together for a common purpose. Fix other areas next. Coach and implement development skills after organizational health issues have improved.

I LOW HEALTH - LOW P2

ASSESSMENT:

Acutely or chronically unhealthy

Issues are not addressed

Low Performance and Productivity, low Wealth

STRATEGIES:

Improve Health first

Organizational Development & Skills Training next

Figure 10: Organizational: QI: Low Health, Low Productivity and Performance

QUADRANT II: LOW HEALTH, HIGH P2

FOR THE ORGANIZATION:

This organization is a high producing, top-notch, public-traded company. While the company was originally a pioneer, it has been well-known for its motto: the outcome justifies the means, ALWAYS... Gradually, although the company appears to continue to produce at a high level, back-stabbing and unethical competition prevails. While some try their best to produce and succeed by competing in a "clean" way, it doesn't take long for other employees to realize that the only way to succeed is to play the game in a risky way to prevail in an unethical organization. Disgusted, some will stay in golden handcuffs in the organization as their lifestyles now "depend" on their income in this company. Others will plan their stay on a temporary basis and will simultaneously plan their transition out. Some will stay for as long as they want, as they are eager to make more money and feel comfortable with the competing parameters...

ASSESSMENT: Similarly to individuals, organizations in this category may be both acutely or chronically affected, although they may continue to produce at a high level. Although business owners, employers, and managers may be reluctant to intervene at this stage, living in the illusion that because performance and productivity continue to be high, everything else must be working well, excessive signs of stress in the organization will be noticeable and expressed in different ways: i.e. employee turnover, increased violence in the workplace, absenteeism, or ethical problems. These may be symptoms of underlying organizational health problems.

STRATEGIES: Improve the organization's health first. Identify the dimensions with the most challenges first and attempt to fix those as a priority. Fix other areas next.

II LOW HEALTH - HIGH P2

ASSESSMENT:

Acute or chronic lack of Health

Unaddressed problems

High Performance and Productivity, High Wealth

STRATEGIES:

Improve Health. Evaluate and fix problems

Manage stress in the workplace.

Figure 11: Organizational: QII: Low Health, High Productivity and Performance

QUADRANT III: HIGH HEALTH, HIGH P2

FOR THE ORGANIZATION:

Everything seems to be working well in this organization. The organization has just launched a new product and it was an immediate boom worldwide. This strategy was well thought out with active participation from every team involved. Although there were some difficulties along the way, there was outstanding pre-planning and leadership in working together through the anticipated challenges. The company learned from a failed launch years before, resulting in a disaster with massive layoff and turnover. Looking ahead, it is preparing itself for some difficulties that don't fully depend upon the organization itself. Although the launch sets up the tone for great growth, the company knows it cannot sit on its glory and needs to actively plan for what is to come. All teams are thriving; with an excellent attitude, they look up to their leader for guidance and they are proud of their own input in the overall process..."

ASSESSMENT: In this quadrant, the organization is healthy or has health related issues under control. The organization maintains a high level of performance and productivity.

STRATEGIES: Identify the healthy strategies and continue to use them to continue your organizational health and wealth. Establish specific goals to continue to improve within each and every area. If your organization is in this quadrant, take the opportunity to grow, invest, and go to the next level. Implement new opportunities one at a time. Organizationally: people will be thriving with a great attitude in place; time in which the organization may want to look at everything in terms of the "whole picture";

maximize productivity and efficiency; one thing at a time; continue to explore new opportunities; maintain acquired level of achievement before moving on to the next level.

III HIGH HEALTH-
HIGH P2

ASSESSMENT:

Healthy organization. Fixes issues as they arise. High Productivity and Performance

STRATEGIES:

Identify and continue to use successful strategies for Health and Wealth. Establish goals to continue to improve in each and every area on an ongoing basis

Figure 12: Organizational: QIII: High Health, High Productivity and Performance

QUADRANT IV: HIGH HEALTH, LOW P2

FOR THE ORGANIZATION:

This is a healthy organization. It has everything in place: a good structure, excellent people, and a great business plan. This young organization is breaking into a new niche, with big competitors in other areas and yet there is still a well-defined new opportunity. There is some impatience in being able to break into the novel business and, at the same time, everyone within the company knows they are on the right track and it is just a question of time and effort...

Assessment: In this quadrant, the organization is healthy or has health related issues under control. The organization has a low level of performance and productivity. This may be a new organization, an organization in transition, or an organization undergoing drastic change.

Strategies: Identify the healthy strategies and continue to use them to continue your organizational health and wealth. Review your business plan. Establish specific goals to improve productivity and performance. Identify opportunities and implement a proactive plan to achieve the desired goals to increase productivity, performance, and improve wealth.

IV HIGH HEALTH-
LOW P2

ASSESSMENT:

Healthy organization but performing poorly

STRATEGIES:

Healthy structure is in place. Develop sound business plan and improve Performance Skills Training. Further Education. Establish a plan for improvement

Figure 13: Organizational: QIV: High Health, Low Productivity and Performance

IN SUMMARY: ORGANIZATIONAL HEALTH & WEALTH STRATEGIES

If your organization is in:

QUADRANT I: LOW HEALTH & LOW P2

Improve the health within your organization first and then implement your business strategies.

QUADRANT II: LOW HEALTH & HIGH P2

Improve the health within your organization first. Identify the dimensions with most challenges first and attempt to fix those as a priority. Fix other dimensions next.

QUADRANT III: HIGH HEALTH & HIGH P2

Identify the healthy strategies and continue to use them to continue your organizational health and wealth. Establish specific goals to continue to improve within each and every area. Take advantage of the opportunity to grow, invest, and go to the next level.

QUADRANT IV: HIGH HEALTH & LOW P2

Identify the healthy strategies and continue to use them to continue your organizational health. Establish specific goals to improve productivity and performance to increase wealth.

LEADING UNDER PRESSURE
Organizational Strategies

	LOW HEALTH HIGH P2 **IMPROVE HEALTH** **II**	HIGH HEALTH HIGH P2 **CONTINUOUS IMPROVEMENT** **III**
PERFORMANCE & PRODUCTIVITY	**I** LOW HEALTH LOW P2 **HEALTH/ BUSINESS**	**IV** HIGH HEALTH LOW P2 **BUSINESS/ EDUCATION**

THE HEALTH CONTINUUM

Figure 14: Organizational: Leading Under Pressure

MAXIMIZE YOUR PERFORMANCE AND PRODUCTIVITY: EFFECTIVE STRATEGIES TO MANAGE YOUR DAILY ROUTINE

STRATEGY #1: ASSESS YOUR CURRENT SITUATION

You have now mastered the individual and organizational strategy quadrants of *Leading Under Pressure*. On the other hand, you won't get very far if you do not know exactly where you stand in your point of departure. Or worse, you can get quite far and will most likely get lost, far, far away from home as you blindly move on your path. The best explorers are always well-prepared even as they go into an unknown, exciting, and uncertain expedition. Yet, through history, we clearly see how these magnificent pioneers brought their essential tools and an unremitting spirit that would prevail in the most dangerous circumstances.

Understanding your current situation, both at home as well as at work and in each and every aspect of your life, is essential toward establishing exactly where you are and where you want to be in the next month, six months, year, or years from now. Going with the flow may sometimes bring some unexpected blessings, but leaving our lives to fate is not necessarily the best way to go!

So what is this decision-making process about? Should we assess each moment of our lives and become robotic players in the major game? Systematizing activities that require a certain and repetitive skill will increase our chances of success, as we can then devote more time and focus on resolving more complex problems. Analyzing your current situation with your personal, professional, and occupational strengths and weaknesses, opportunities and challenges is vital for your next steps and strategic interventions. As the chess-player makes sure to have a board and all the pieces in the right place prior to a match, you must account for your tools, including all the critical parts – capabilities and skills – which will enable you to effectively play the corporate game at the highest level and succeed!

Chances are you are, just as I am, the ever-accomplishing juggler, taking more and more responsibilities at work and at home, wanting it all and not giving anything up. Well, let me tell you, we still haven't figured out how to stretch our days into 24+ hour days, but a law may be passed anytime soon! Imagine having a week of 5 days of... let me do the math... 33 hours each, and we could have a free half day per week... Well, let me shake you up a bit, come back to reality, and then think about how you and I are going to effectively mix and match all those "must-do" activities with "may do" and "would like to do" actions as we are, indeed, striving for the gold!

So now, you have a great idea! And, as you are busy in your other thousand chores and responsibilities, you start building a new world in your mind's eye. And your vision becomes stronger and stronger, and you are already feeling the thrill of this thought, which is now also manifesting within yourself with the warm feeling of chocolate milk and cookies. And now the thoughts and feelings are also felt as energy in your body, as you feel the rush of creation manifesting on the physical dimension at its best. And the more you think about your idea and the more you feel it in your emotional sphere and in your body, you start giving it some shape in your spiritual being as well as transform it in the impact your idea will have when it comes to existence in the tangible plane within your world. You have just created a new possibility and it is up to you to bring it from your mind's eye into the physical world!

Wouldn't it be great if we were able to create and execute one idea at a time? Yet, a novel inspiration may prove itself dangerous in the life of the busy executive as she/he has multiple and diverse responsibilities and now, this great idea becomes a thorn in the path of a hectic schedule. Now, as an executive, you start feeling the pain of wishing to pursue your new idea, yet realizing your pile of things "to do!" You start thinking of the positives and negatives of continuing things as they are versus implementing the new, great idea that you have just created. You have a zillion things to do and this idea is creeping up in your mind until you feel you are about to explode in a big bang of creation! The inevitable happens. You have decided to bring your will power to its maximum power, you are ready to take this new venture head on and make it happen!

This is a great opportunity to take a step back, a big step back, take a deep breath, and take a closer look at what your week really looks like. If you are efficient at keeping good track of your daily activities and responsibilities, take a closer look at your calendar. If you don't, grab pencil and paper and mark down everything that you do throughout the course of the day: **EVERYTHING.** This is your opportunity to check on how it is that you spend your day at work and at home. Once you have written it all down – meeting times, interactive times with clients, employees, colleagues, students, teachers, spouse, children, parents, siblings and friends, activities and everything – then lay out your "playing map" and see exactly where you stand in your maze of life. Aha! So, you HAVE created a day with more hours, how could you possibly have been doing all of this and how can you even think of squeezing in anything else?

The most effective strategies I've found include the ability to conceptualize, think, and plan ahead of the game before actually going into action. This simple task provides for the opportunity to find the best and shortest way to reach our goals. In an efficient system, instead of going through five steps, we can instead bypass one or two steps and just go straight to the next one. If we allow ourselves to observe from a more global perspective, we can see which steps we can or cannot skip to achieve our goals.

STRATEGY #2: ESTABLISH YOUR GOALS

Identify the positives and the negatives of each activity you are about to undertake. If you want to go from point A to E, I would suggest that you look into the positives (pros) or negatives (cons) of going through each step first. This will help prioritize needs and wants. Once this has been decided, it is then appropriate to establish a path toward reaching your well-thought-out goals. You may also look into performing a SWOT analysis, looking at the Strengths, Weaknesses, Opportunities, and Threats of each major endeavor you are to undertake.

SMART GOALS, first described by Locke and Latham in their motivational theory and modified over time with practical add-ons, include the need for goals to be specific, measurable and motivating, achievable and attainable, realistic and relevant, tangible and traceable through time. You can easily apply this strategic approach in improving and achieving a higher level in your work performance and productivity as well as in your health and wellbeing.

STRATEGY #3: CREATE YOUR STRATEGY

As an integral part of your strategic planning, you will need to identify how you spend most of your time and how you perceive most of your activities.

- **MUST DO - ACTIVITIES** are those activities that only you can do. Only you can be the spouse, only you can be the mother or father, only you can be the business owner, manager, or employee. I continuously see people falling in the trap of perceiving all of their activities within this area, taking away other options or opportunities. **Common traps:** leaving little, if any, time for you.

- **MAY DO - ACTIVITIES** are those activities in which you do have a choice; you may decide whether or not the action needs to take place and you can also decide whether only you can execute the activity or whether you can have someone else perform this activity. This is the area where most people need to work on: to allow them to delegate to others who may or may not perform the activity itself with the same precision or perfection. It is essential to identify delegating opportunities in this area. **Common traps:** not delegating anything or staying in limbo, not doing anything at all.

- **WOULD LIKE TO DO - ACTIVITIES** are activities which we desire and choose to do. **Common traps:** overindulgence.

STRATEGY #4: PRIORITIZE YOUR DAILY SCHEDULE

1. Plan your life and your business, particularly what is routine.
2. Create a schedule AND STICK TO IT.
3. Keep a master calendar. Anticipate areas in which you may add activities. Avoid double- or triple-booking (redundant, isn't it?).
4. Organize and plan all regular assignments and activities ahead of time.
5. Designate specific notebooks for specific projects. Keep an organized outline.
6. Avoid unnecessary interruptions. If you are pressured by a deadline as you are preparing a report, avoid answering emails or calls that will distract your full attention and delay the completion of your current project. If you feel the need to "multitask," listen to music.
7. Use checklists, particularly if you feel inundated by multiple requests. Work on threes, complete and check the first three activities you need to do by order of priority and then move on to the next three.
8. Revise your list. Discard whatever has been repeatedly left in the back burner. If you haven't completed the activity for one year, decide whether it needs to be done at all. Delegate it if you still feel the action needs to take place, or delete it completely from your list if you decide it is no longer relevant. Let go: do not hold on to things you are not going to do: create "good space" to allow good opportunities to come your way.
9. Prepare for the day or week ahead. This will provide for a good sense of being ready for the challenges.
10. Provide necessary support, mentoring, coaching, or

work with others. Delegate as needed.

11. Remember: you and your loved ones come first.

STRATEGY #5: HAVE MEETINGS THAT WORK FOR YOU

As an example, a common complaint I often hear is executives, professionals, and entrepreneurs feel swamped with endless meetings with no tangible outcome. Going through nonstop processes does not necessarily allow for the allocated time to get things done! Although planning is an essential component that needs to take place prior to undertaking a given activity, micromanaging activities or discussing processes forever won't necessarily ensure the final product will be any better than if you had just focused on achieving your goal directly. My suggestion: first consider having a meeting that has a regular schedule, i.e. a meeting once a week should probably not take more than an hour. Extraordinary meetings, strategic planning meetings, or development meetings should be scheduled and planned for in advance. Any meeting should have the following three key components:

- **Beginning:** There should be a previously designated leader, coordinator, or moderator during each meeting. The purpose of the meeting (the agenda) should be addressed in advance. There should be up to three general objectives for the meeting. The meeting agenda should have been sent to each member at least a day prior to the meeting, in the early stages. As you organize your future meetings, the agenda for the next meeting should be included in the meeting summary.

- **Middle:** After addressing the key points to be discussed, all participants should have time to discuss each objective. Moderating meetings is an art. As a rule of thumb, though, if only challenges are brought up, it is imperative to also suggest potential solutions. Having some tangible ways of addressing problem issues will leave everyone with a good sense of accomplishment, whereas discussing only the challenges will leave everyone feeling frustrated. Summarize at least three points for each objective that resulted from the discussion.

- **End:** Outline the conclusions, address the action items to be performed during the course of the week, establish timelines, and identify those responsible for completing each task. Summarize the meeting in the following format and provide for the summary and the following meeting's agenda:

  - Meeting objectives (three to five),
  - Discussion points: same points and any additional point brought up in the beginning, three key points within each one.
  - Conclusions, action items, and deadlines. Outline three objectives for the following meeting.

STRATEGY #6: STICK TO TIMELINES

If you are about to create and implement a plan, it is imperative you conceptualize this plan across time. Many will design a great plan but will disregard the importance of following this plan in terms of time. I see many companies spending thousands of dollars in a one-time intervention, writing a check on "done" but not necessarily benefiting from the investment. Consider the following outline for any plan that requires some behavioral modification, whether you are starting a new diet, an exercise schedule, a relaxation exercise, an educational program, a development plan for an employee, or a master-plan for yourself:

1. When starting a new plan, check it on a weekly basis for the first month on days 7, 14, 21, and 28.
2. Write the check-up times on your calendar.
3. Evaluate your improvement, fine tune, and continue.
4. After the 28th day, move on to a monthly planning mode at days 30, 60, 90, 180, and 360.
5. Continue yearly planning thereafter, particularly if everything is going well and you have learned self-assessment strategies and you can implement ongoing improvement.

- **WEEKLY PLANNING:** Days 7, 14, 21, 28
- **MONTHLY PLANNING:** Days 30, 60, 90, 180, 360
- **YEARLY PLANNING:** Yearly thereafter

I address more strategies and the creation of a comprehensive plan for improvement in *Managing Work in Life*.

CHAPTER 14

MAXIMIZE YOUR PERFORMANCE AND PRODUCTIVITY: EFFECTIVE STRATEGIES TO MANAGE CRISES

As successful business leaders, professionals, managers, or employees, many of us feel like we are in the "spinning 24/7 wheel". We wake up with a full schedule of things "to do," at the same time that we juggle our personal and our family's activities while working. This art may be mastered to the smallest detail until some unexpected event throws us off course. How do we continue conducting business as usual while dealing with a crisis? Regardless of where we live – hurricane-stricken areas, earthquake-prone ones, or man-made instigated ones – being prepared is essential to our survival and success. While unexpected events may be catastrophic in nature, it is the emotional intensity that may overwhelm our senses (and good judgment) during those challenging times. Coping with personal loss, whether it is the loss of a close friend, a family member, divorce, or financial difficulties, will add to the emotional turmoil while continuing to run business "as usual." The following are general strategies I have found effective in my work as a consultant in crisis management, as a medical doctor, as well as in my own experience as a business owner.

STRATEGY #1: ASSESS THE SITUATION

If you are facing an unexpected event, whether it ranges from a catastrophic-like event to the loss of a significant family member or friend, ensure your own safety, your family's safety, and the safety of those who work with you. You cannot blink in choosing people first. Our thoughts are expressed into words and transformed into actions. Ensure that what you think and say match your actions. If you believe there is an emergency and tell the world that you are in an emergency situation and, instead, you continue other ongoing activities of less relevance, what you are saying does not match what you are doing. Make sure your thoughts and words align with your behavior. Establish a "range of emergency situations," so as to react accordingly. Keep things in perspective: look at the whole picture and avoid interpreting crises as overwhelming.

STRATEGY #2: CONCENTRATE ON THE "HERE AND NOW"

Take care of yourself on a regular basis. You will be able to respond to a crisis if you are in a good place to begin with. Ground yourself. Find exactly where you stand during the critical moment. If you have a plan in place, go to it immediately and get everyone involved. Assign activities and actions to everyone and lead the way to resolving the situation assertively and steadily. If you do not have a plan in place, create a crisis team and work through the crisis together. Organize the discussions so as to resolve the problem together, take note, and use as a template for future planning.

STRATEGY #3: GO BACK TO YOUR SCHEDULE OR PLAN AS SOON AS POSSIBLE

Start with the simplest routine; make sure your "Four Pillars of Biological Health" plan is in place. Break it down to small steps if needed. Go back to your business plan. This plan should be easily available as during times of crisis or personal loss, or both, it may be difficult to "remember" exactly what the next step was. Maintain a positive attitude about your ability to solve the situation. Look for opportunities to grow beyond just resolving the problem. Make relevant decisions that relate to your here and now. Move forward as you immerse yourself in change. Resisting it will slow down the flow whereas sailing with inevitable change will bring about novel opportunities.

STRATEGY #4: AVOID MAKING BIG CHANGES DURING TIMES OF CRISIS

If you need to make some changes in your business, make sure you go through the critical thinking process during the successful resolution of the critical situation. Avoid making drastic changes during the critical time. Many feel the temptation to make all the changes they may have fantasized for quite some time. Take the time to conduct a quick assessment of positive or negative outcomes with each action you want to undertake. With more time, conduct a SWOT analysis, addressing the strengths and weaknesses, opportunities and threats of each further action.

STRATEGY #5: APPROACH YOUR TRUSTED CIRCLE

Build your supportive network in times of "peace." Many have shared with me they were not at their best intellectual ability during times of tremendous stress and believe they made poor decisions they later regretted. Learn exactly what each of your employees, colleagues, and friends can offer. While some may offer their emotional support or be good listeners, others may offer their advice and help you make the decisions. Avoid isolating yourself and allow yourself to collaborate with others who may also be going through a hard time as well. You'd be surprised how many people around you may be willing to help you if you only asked.

STRATEGY #6: ESTABLISH SIGNIFICANT RELATIONSHIPS BEYOND YOUR COMFORT GROUP

Having an extended networking group will assist you in your swift recovery, as you will continue to be in touch with others who may share common goals, as well as collaborate with others who may need your products or services. Move toward your goals on an individual level and see how you can cross-collaborate with others to maximize everybody's benefit. Think about contacting three people you know on a daily basis as you are trying to bounce back from the critical situation.

STRATEGY #7: ASSESS YOUR INTERVENTION

Evaluate what worked and what didn't work for you. Improve your overall plan and plan ahead. Consider this an opportunity to continue to improve your business and to simplify as much of the process as possible. While many expect a magic solution to resolve a time of crisis, the most effective strategies still consist of being consistently organized on a regular basis. Keep hope alive. As entrepreneurs leading your companies, or executives leading and managing your work group, others will look up to you to lead them during times of crisis. This does not mean you have to do it alone. Share your hope and concerns with others as you move forward. This sharing will not only inspire others but will refuel your own energy as you move forward.

CHAPTER 15

EFFECTIVE STRATEGIES TO MAXIMIZE YOUR HEALTH & WELLBEING: THE FOUR PILLARS OF BIOLOGICAL HEALTH

We manifest our mission into action within the physical dimension. Busy entrepreneurs, road warriors, and corporate executives are challenged with accomplishing more with less, stretching their biological systems to the max. Although we may be able to exert amazing levels of power, our physical systems may give in if confronted with ongoing challenges and without finding the right times to recover our energy. The four biological pillars that contribute to wellbeing are: nutrition, sleep, exercise, and relaxation. Maximizing your performance within each of these will enable you endure the ups and downs of dealing with personal and corporate challenges. I am often asked about a "magical" recipe for dealing with crisis situations. The biological strategy in the physical dimension is to maximize biology on a regular basis. This simple premise will help you bounce back to a good, healthy lifestyle during challenging times.

STRATEGY #1: MAXIMIZE YOUR NUTRITION

Good nutrition is a key pillar providing for our physical, mental, and emotional stamina. There are too many guidelines as to "what" to eat, but few to guide as to "how" to eat healthy. The bottom line is simple: implementing a healthy diet demands discipline and adhesion to a schedule. Balancing carbohydrates, fats, and protein is key and will depend upon each individual. As a rule of thumb, consider breakfast, lunch, a snack, and dinner, as the essential structure of a healthy diet. Considering an additional couple of healthy snacks may be plenty for the busy executive and entrepreneur, only if complemented with daily exercise. As a general rule, consider dividing the "awake" day in even intervals, say, four-hour intervals. Meal times ought to be included in your schedule, just as you would include a business meeting, or an appointment to hire a new employee. A thirty minute break if you can eat at your facility will suffice. Consider meal times as sacred: sit down and concentrate on your meal rather than eat while you are checking on your email or catching up with work. If you are eating alone at work, listen to music or allow yourself to relax. Otherwise, take the time to eat with a colleague. A ten minute break for a snack may suffice as well, using the same strategy. Eat with your family at home. Not only will this enhance your relationship with your loved ones, there is sufficient evidence showing that children who have dinner with their parents are smarter and do better in school.

Many are more eager to fill their bodies with multiple vitamins and over-the-counter potions rather than in eating well. The Mediterranean diet incorporates the basic components of healthy eating, including fruits and vegetables, fish and whole grains. Add olive oil and a glass of red wine and you will be well underway in living a healthy diet providing the stamina for your heart and your brain. If you want to take vitamins, consider taking one multivitamin a day. Nothing replaces good eating habits and eating healthy food.

Avoid drinking more than two cups of coffee a day and

avoid drinking coffee or caffeinated drinks after 2 p.m. Espresso is more aromatic and, believe it or not, contains less caffeine than drip coffee. If you do not drink alcohol, do not start. One glass of wine at night may help you improve your health but avoid drinking more than two. Red wine contains antioxidants known as flavonoids which may protect against heart disease. Additionally, red wine contains resveratrol, a substance that may reduce the risk for blood clots. Although most professionals and executives don't tend to drink alcohol during work hours in the United States, many consider drinking wine with their meals while conducting business in other parts of the world acceptable and desirable. Avoid drinking more than two beers or a hard drink on a regular basis. Remember, if you are already experiencing trouble with the negative cycle of coffee and alcohol, or if you are experiencing signs and symptoms of depression or anxiety, you may want to avoid these altogether.

STRATEGY #2: MAXIMIZE YOUR EXERCISE

Exercise is another essential component of the formula to stay physically fit and healthy. Morning exercise is the most effective, relaxing, and energizing. Morning exercise will allow you to start off fresh, increase your blood flow, increase your metabolism, and produce natural endorphins (neurotransmitters that make you feel good and decrease your pain perception). After exercising, your body may feel pleasantly relaxed physically, while mentally sharp, focused, and clear. Relaxing exercises tend to be the most repetitive (and boring) ones: walking, cycling, running, jogging, spinning, cross-country skiing, and swimming. Some use this exercise time to think and plan, taking advantage of the relaxed mental state while exercising. These are excellent exercises (and a must!) for busy executives and entrepreneurs who spend hours of sedentary work and for those who fly and travel as a part of their busy schedules. If you anticipate a more demanding work schedule, consider challenging yourself by increasing your strength. Weight lifting or increased resistance exercises will enable you to increase strength. Alternate aerobic with weight lifting exercises. Consider exercising daily. The American Medical Association suggests a minimum of thirty minutes of daily exercise.

STRATEGY #3: MAXIMIZE YOUR SLEEP

Sleep is the third pillar of biological health. Many minimize the benefits of sleep and the essential properties sleep brings to our ability to produce and perform at a high level. Sleep dysregulation and stress can increase the risk for depression and anxiety. These problems may also have direct influence over the immune system and increase the risk for heart disease. Stressed corporate warriors, professionals, and entrepreneurs carry their worries and concerns to their sleep. As they can't relax and reenergize throughout the course of the night, many wake up tired and exhausted, unable to focus, further prolonging the negative cycle. In short: they are stressed out during the course of the day and stressed out during the course of the night. In contrast, sleeping six to eight hours every night will enhance your physical, intellectual, and emotional stamina. Having a "good night sleep" will improve your ability to concentrate during the course of the day, gaining control over activities and responsibilities.

Additionally, sleep regulation is a must for anyone experiencing signs and symptoms of depression or anxiety. Avoid back-to-back red-eye travel and accommodate to the new time zone schedule as quickly as possible.

STRATEGY #4: MAXIMIZE YOUR RELAXATION

Relaxation strategies compose the fourth pillar of biological health. Sleep and exercise have a direct impact on enhancing a relaxed state. Additionally, guided imagery, visualization techniques, meditation, and listening to music are powerful tools against physical signs of stress. These strategies include the ability to create a state of calm at the start of the day, anticipating activities or events with the opportunity to resolve situations throughout the day. Practicing relaxation techniques on a regular basis adds to the strategic armamentarium of the traveling executive, providing beneficial lasting effects in brain activity and the immune system. You may want to maximize the use of relaxation techniques in the morning, throughout the course of the day, as needed, and in the evening. Taking a few minutes to yourself may help some. Others benefit more from taking a couple of periods throughout the day. Times for relaxation range from five minutes twice a day to thirty minutes once to more times throughout the course of the day. Winding down toward the evening will enable you to sleep better at night as well. Listen to music or book audiotapes daily while you drive; meditate or use guided imagery exercises daily when you are awake, during breaks, at night, or while you travel (and when you are not driving). Although there are numerous relaxation techniques that you may want to practice, the most common induction techniques usually begin with deep breathing exercises. Progressive relaxation and guided imagery techniques share a common general outline. The more you practice, the deeper state of relaxation you will achieve. If you are interested in learning more about guided imagery relaxation exercises, please visit our website under Resources: **Quantum Wellbeing at www.ExecutiveHealthWealth.com/resources.html**

STRATEGY #5: BE IN THE HERE AND NOW

It is vital to concentrate on each activity, one at a time, at the present moment, rather than driving in the car, listening to music, answering to business calls on the cellular phone while writing on a pad, eating a sandwich and punching in numbers to a PDA, all while driving! In essence, the trick is to "be in the here and now," and nowhere else. My experience in the wide spectrum of scenarios along wellness and disease has guided me to understand that it is those people who can be "busy on the outside, calm on the inside" who can truly create an integrated state of wellbeing.

To learn more about the "Four Pillars of Biological Health," please read *Managing Work in Life*.

INDIVIDUAL HEALTH & ORGANIZATIONAL HEALTH

To get things done, it is essential to look at the following areas to effectively manage work in life for our personal, professional, and organizational well-being:

From an individual perspective, one of the most obvious and important areas is the

- **Physical dimension:** The Four Pillars of Biological Health: Nutrition, sleep, exercise, and relaxation practices. This is where the **mission** that we have designed for ourselves manifests on the physical plane.
- Next is the **emotional dimension.** This is the area where our ability to connect with others resides. Our relationships with family and friends make our affective world rich and joyful.
- Our **cognitive or intellectual dimension** is next. In this area there is training, education, and the constant learning skills from a mental perspective. This is the area where our vision for the future is created.
- The next area has to do with **social life and behavior.** As a person, our well-being and growth also depends on our ability to connect and inter-relate with our community, our work organization, and other organizations and cultures.
- Lastly is the **spiritual dimension**, which includes

our relationship with a higher being or connection with our higher self through prayer, meditation, and self-awareness. This area includes voluntarism, altruism, and esthetics. This is the key area where our values reside. Our individual ethics connect to our **value system** within this area.

All of these dimensions are essential components of the healthy lifestyle and interact in dynamic processes. **Productivity and performance** processes operate within each of these areas, allowing us to constantly improve within each dimension.

HEALTHY LIFESTYLE

Physical	Nutrition, Sleep, Exercise, Relaxation, **MISSION**
Emotional	Relationship with Family and Friends
Cognitive	Constant Learning, Skills Training, **VISION**
Social	Community, Family Organization, Social Support
Spiritual	Prayer, Meditation, Ethics, Volunteerism, Altruism , Aesthetics. **VALUES**
Performance	Quality of work, Self - assessment and feedback evaluation
Productivity	Work Output, Compensation

Figure 15: The Healthy Lifestyle

The above descriptions apply to a personal or individual perspective, but we can use the same framework in regards to a **healthy organization:**

- Within the **physical dimension** I would include the safety, the structure, and the human element we choose for our organization, whether it's our own company or a multinational corporation. This is also where the organizational **mission-in-action** is brought to life.
- The **emotional dimension** of a healthy organization includes the corporate culture-openness and trust, the ability to receive feedback, and sustain employee hope during critical times.
- The **intellectual dimension** within an organization includes the training, the learning, and the skills training necessary to constantly improve within the organization. This is where the **vision for the organization** is created.
- The **social dimension** includes the community involvement of an organization and the relationship that it creates with other corporations, cultures, and organizations.
- In the **spiritual dimension**, the healthy organization's values compose the foundation of the organization. **Ethical values**, voluntarism, and altruism are key components within this area at the organizational level.

As in the individual healthy lifestyle, all of these dimensions are intimately related and interact in dynamic processes. **Performance and productivity** within each dimension bring in the dynamic processes within each area, providing for the opportunity for constant improvement. The more aligned the individual dimensions are with the corresponding organizational dimensions, the better the relationship between the individual and his or her organization. The better alignment there is, the better the match, the better the chances of maximum productivity, performance, and longstanding well-being.

HEALTHY
ORGANIZATION

Physical	Safety, Structure, Human element, **MISSION** IN ACTION
Emotional	Corporate Culture, openness, trust, feedback
Cognitive	Training, Constant Learning, Skills Training, **VISION**
Social	Community Involvement, Relationship with environment
Spiritual	Ethics, Volunteerism, Altruism , Aesthetics, **VALUES**
Performance	Quality of product or services, Self -assessment and feedback evaluation and constant improvement
Productivity	Work Output, Wealth

Figure 16: The Healthy Organization

D r. Gabý Corá is president and founder of the **Executive Health & Wealth Institute®** and managing partner of the **Florida Neuroscience Center**. She's author of *The Power of Wellbeing®: Leading Under Pressure* (2007), *Managing Work in Life®,* and *Quantum Wellbeing.* She's also author of the *Alpha Leader Series*, beginning with the provocative *Alpha Female* (2008). She has a unique set of skills: Dr. Corá is a licensed medical doctor with a master's in business administration, board certified psychiatrist and trained mediator. Her energized enthusiasm, strategic focus, and innovative style are qualities in action as a corporate consultant, wellness coach, and expert speaker, making her a key collaborator of Fortune 500 companies and international organizations. Dr. Corá has worked with C-level executives and entrepreneurs, assisting them in crisis leadership, strategic planning, cultural proficiency, health and wellness in the workplace, and life-work management. She has consulted and given presentations in North and South America, Europe, Africa, and Asia. She integrates a unique combination of capabilities: a strong foundation of knowledge, twenty years of experience, and an intuitive deductive ability. She's Fellow of the American Psychiatric Association and a Board Director of the American Psychiatric Foundation. She lectures at the Executive MBA at the University of Miami, School of Business; she's a Professional Member of the National Speakers Association, and a regular guest on radio and television shows speaking on health and wellness. She has been interviewed in CNN, Fox News, *The New York Times, Chicago Tribune, Forbes, Business Week, and Women Entrepreneur.*

Prior to EH&WI, she was Director, Regional Medical Research Specialist, at Pfizer Pharmaceuticals, serving as the Southeast Regional Council Coordinator and its representative to the sales department. Throughout her career at Pfizer, she was deeply involved in facilitating strategic business planning, effective teambuilding, mentoring, and coaching others individually and in teams, receiving the 2000 Pfizer Values in Action Award for Teamwork. Prior to Pfizer, she was a Clinical Research Associate at the prestigious National Institutes of Health, serving as Lieutenant Commander in the US Public Health Service, where she was elected Chair of the Hispanic Officers' Advisory Committee to the Surgeon General. As a clinical researcher, she headed the Obsessive-Compulsive Disorder Unit Research Clinic, building a highly specialized clinical team and conducting state-of-the-art clinical research, which resulted in cutting-edge treatment options and peer-reviewed publications. She received the Hannah Cashman Memorial Award in recognition for her dedicated and compassionate care given by the Consultation Liaison service at NIMH. Dr. Corá pursued a research career after her residency in Psychiatry at Saint Elizabeths' Hospital, in Washington, DC. Most people know she became a doctor in 1989. Few people know she was twenty-four, graduating with a nine month-old and a twenty-five month-old, with honors. Dr. Corá built a successful professional career while she built her personal family life with her husband and children. She is fluent in English, Spanish, and French and appears in *Who's Who in Executives & Professionals, Who's Who in Medicine and Healthcare, Who's Who in America, and Who's Who in the World.*

BY DR. GABY CORÁ

MANAGING WORK IN LIFE

If we lived in an ideal world, we would live by the rule of thirds. First, we would work eight hours of the day. Next, we would spend eight hours in recreational activities. Last, but not least, in the ideal world, we would recover our energy by sleeping eight hours every night, refreshing our bodies and minds, to start a new day with plenty of energy and stamina.

Managing Work in Life will assist you:

- Understand the Myth of Life-Work Balance
- Learn about the Healthy Individual and the Healthy Organization
- Learn a Seven Step Plan to achieve your goals while mastering your New Life Business Plan®

QUANTUM WELLBEING

A groundbreaking program that integrates Dr. Corá's years of experience as a medical doctor and business consultant, **QUANTUM WELLBEING I:** *The Core*, is the first in the series of meditation and relaxation exercises available for busy executives, road warriors, and entrepreneurs. Dr. Corá facilitates *The Core* using progressive relaxation techniques and guided imagery as you **discover your source of energy: creating a strong core to enjoy enduring success. Quantum Wellbeing** will enhance your health and wellbeing at the deepest level.

When can I use Quantum Wellbeing?

- When you are experiencing high levels of stress
- When you are having trouble sleeping
- When you feel worried about flying
- When you are extremely tired and ready for a nap but need to keep going with work
- When you want your body to relax but your mind to stay focused

ALPHA FEMALE
Leader Of A Pack Of Bitches
Winning Strategies To Become An
Outstanding Leader

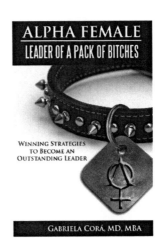

Everyone has had that kind of female boss, the one that you think inappropriate words for when she gets to that time of the month or starts emotional wars during the busiest projects of the day. Some days it's just better to stand back and let her attack someone else, but other days you just can't stay out of the line of fire. What do you do when your female boss is acting like a, well, bitch?

ALPHA FEMALE is aimed directly at both female leaders and the people they rule. No man will dare say the things Dr. Gaby Corá says in her book: although they are politically incorrect for a man to say, a woman leader can certainly get away with stating the truth.

ALPHA FEMALE describes what most men think but don't dare say and what many women know but avoid altogether.

TELL IT AS IT IS:

FIVE USEFUL TIPS FOR MEN & WOMEN STRIVING TO SURVIVE ALPHA FEMALES:

- STAY AWAY If you can't stay away,
- SIT If you can't sit,

- GO FETCH If you can't go fetch,
- PLAY DEAD If you can't play dead,
- READ THIS BOOK!

Order your Copy of Alpha Female Today!
Call 1-866-762-7632 or Visit us Online at
www.ExecutiveHealthWealth.com

BURNOUT: DO YOU NEED A COACH OR A DOCTOR?

"Stress is the buzzword of the twenty-first century," Dr. Gabriela Corá recently said on Fox News. In her new book, *Leading Under Pressure*, she addresses the multiple challenges corporate executives and entrepreneurs face as they strive to achieve higher goals with increased competition, progressively limited resources, and the same manpower. "Burnt-out, energy-depleted, or constantly stressed, many find themselves unable to take pleasure in their hard-earned position," Dr. Corá says.

As a strategic solution, Dr. Corá suggests to use a matrix approach looking at the ability to produce wealth and the interaction with the state of health. "It is the corporate executives and business owners who still operate at a high level of performance and productivity but struggle with keeping their minds and bodies healthy that will eventually exhaust their biological stamina, and potentially burn out," she says.

Many companies, executives, and entrepreneurs have hired coaches - many of whom left their own corporate jobs because of burnout - to help increase performance at work. "While efficiency may be helpful to maximize our ability to produce, coaches may not be as helpful when the person is already pumping their energy with plenty of coffee during the day and having trouble sleeping at night without the use of alcoholic beverages or hypnotics. Many of these successful executives seek to see a doctor when they are already experiencing heartburn, chest pain, or panic attacks. I'd like to see people preventing these physical events from even happening," Dr. Corá says. "People who are experiencing a series of medical issues triggered by stress may not benefit from coaching as much as people who are healthy and want to improve their performance at work. Everyone who is Leading Under Pressure needs to prioritize health, implement treatment as necessary, and improve lifestyle strategies."

Dr. Corá says you will benefit from having a coach if you are performing and producing at a good baseline level and if you want to continue to improve. You will also benefit if you feel somewhat disorganized and need direction in how to prioritize or organize your day. Lastly, you will benefit from a coach if you feel the need of an outside force to keep you on track. On the other hand, you may benefit from having expert assistance if you would like to implement healthy lifestyle strategies and work on improving your performance and productivity, managing work in life and improving in each and every area of your life.

"There is room for both," Dr. Corá says, "It's important to intervene with the right approach. If I was experiencing heart discomfort, I would like to be seen by a cardiologist and not by a dentist. This will save entrepreneurs and executives the precious time they don't have to spare to begin with."

Corporate Consulting Services

Dr. Gaby Corá has assisted executives and entrepreneurs, their teams, and their organizations in a wide range of events. She is expert in assessing, diagnosing, planning, and creating intervention plans in complex situations, including crisis leadership, strategic planning, organizational behavior, health and wellness in the workplace, and work in life management. She has extensive experience coaching entrepreneurs and C-level executives.

Although each of her programs has a blueprint representing its core, she thrives to design and custom-make programs that are uniquely applicable to her clients' needs. Her forte is to offer integrated coaching and seminars at your corporation or designated location for your convenience.

Dr. Gaby Corá prefers to conduct the first consultation in person as she firmly believes nothing beats a face-to-face meeting. Your preference may be to see her at her Miami offices or you may both decide it is best for her to see you in action within your organization. She offers in-person and teleconference consultations and she will travel to join you and your team.

Executive Coaching: Individual and Team Coaching

- Leadership Coaching, Mentoring, and Advising
- Performance and Development Coaching
- Crisis Management Coaching

Seminars & Keynotes

- Leading Under Pressure
- Managing Work in Life
- Quantum Wellbeingtm
- The New Life Business Plan
- Health & Wellness in the Workplace

To Contact Dr. Gaby Cora about her Corporate Consulting and Coaching Services visit us at www.ExecutiveHealthWealth.com or call 1-866-762-7632.

**Gabriela Cora, MD, MBA, President
the Executive Health & Wealth Institute®, Inc
Tel: 305-762-7632 — Toll Free: 1-866-762-7632
www.ExecutiveHealthWealth.com**